UNDERCURRENTS Series Editor Fintan O'Toole

Diverse Communities: The Evolution of Lesbian and Gay Politics in Ireland

KIERAN ROSE

CORK UNIVERSITY PRESS

First published in 1994 by
Cork University Press
University College
Cork
Ireland

© Kieran Rose 1994

British Library Cataloguing in Publication Data

A CIP catalogue record for this book is available from the British Library

ISBN 0 902561 73 1

Typeset in Ireland by Seton Music Graphics Ltd, Co. Cork
Printed in Ireland by ColourBooks, Baldoyle, Co. Dublin

For those who did not survive

CONTENTS

Acknowledgements   *page* ix

1. Introduction   1

2. Stonewall and Before   4

3. Twenty Years a Growing   9

4. Law Reform   34

5. The Future   59

Conclusion   73

Notes   73

Suggestions for Further Reading and Bibliography   76

ACKNOWLEDGEMENTS

I would like to thank Fintan O'Toole and those working at Cork University Press for their patience and encouragement.

Many people too numerous to mention have helped me to write this book but I would particularly like to thank Christopher Robson for his generous contributions. I would also like to thank all the others who contributed including: Eoin Collins, Tom Cooney, Carol Coulter, Jeff Dudgeon, Arthur Leahy, Hubert Mannion, Sheena McCambley, Donal Sheehan, Marie Smyth and Nexus Research for office facilities provided. Any errors are of course my own. The text is largely based on my personal experience in the lesbian and gay movement and in radical politics generally in Cork and Dublin; it is not the dispassionate report of an outside observer. Given the constraints of space, it cannot hope to be a comprehensive account but, hopefully, such studies will be published in the near future.

Kieran Rose
May, 1994

1. INTRODUCTION

On Wednesday 30 June 1993, the Minister for Justice, Máire Geoghegan-Quinn, crossed the floor of the Senate chamber and, smiling broadly, shook hands with the lesbians and gay men in the public gallery. The Seanad had just passed all remaining stages of the Bill decriminalising homosexuality and providing for equality with heterosexuals. Cutting through decades of judicial and political fretting and centuries of criminalisation, the Bill stated with elegant simplicity that 'any rule of law by virtue of which buggery between persons is an offence is hereby abolished'. The same legal regime would now apply to homosexual and heterosexual behaviour with a common age of consent of seventeen years and the same privacy codes. The atmosphere in the Senate during the two-day debate was one of joy, relief and excitement.

For me that handshake symbolised the end of a twenty-year law reform campaign and the beginning of a new relationship between the Irish state and its lesbian and gay community. Over that period the Irish lesbian and gay community, since the establishment of the Irish Gay Rights Movement in the early 1970s, had presented difficult challenges to the legislature and judiciary, police and governments, but also to the universities, media, the churchs, and representative organisations and political groups and parties on the left and right. Some institutions, especially the trade unions, had responded positively and expanded, for example, the principle of solidarity between workers to include the rights of lesbian and gay workers. Many others, especially the more exalted ones such as the judiciary and the universities, were thrown into confusion by the demands of the lesbian and gay movement and reneged on their basic principles. The resulting conflicts raised issues of sexuality, definitions of being Irish, civil rights and the Constitution, the rights of minorities, the role of Church and State, the duty of legislators, of community development and disadvantage. Most of all, they

1

raised the question of what type of society we wanted for the future. Irish society had changed considerably in the twenty-year period and the lesbian and gay community had made considerable progress from a position of almost total marginalisation and powerlessness. During that time it became possible to construct a new identity, which meant that it is possible to be Irish *and* lesbian *and* gay.

In the Dáil the previous week, the Minister spoke of the Bill as being 'a necessary development of human rights', which was based on the principle of equality and which sought to end a form of discrimination against gay people. She described the old legislation as 'grossly and gratuitously offensive' to gay men and any proposal to provide an unequal age of consent was underpinned by 'a genuine lack of understanding of human nature'. The reform was enthusiastically welcomed by all sides of both Houses of the Oireachtas. It was seen as 'one of the historic events of the decade', 'long overdue', 'a great day for Ireland', 'of far-reaching importance', and 'truly liberating'. The contributions were almost without exception well-informed and generous and dealt with the rights of lesbians and gay men, the principles of equality, the nature of sexuality and the duty of legislators to provide for difference. The Minister for Equality and Law Reform, Mervyn Taylor, asked rhetorically 'What could be more important for us as legislators than to create a climate and a space where two people who have chosen each other can express and share their love?'

The Government introduced a law reform in its first months in office and it chose the more radical option, which, in the words of the leaked memo, 'would in effect equate, for the purposes of the law, homosexual and heterosexual behaviour'. There was no sense that these legal rights were being given grudgingly. For a country that was thought to be irredeemably reactionary on sexual-related issues, this was astonishing progress, which has not been sufficiently acknowledged or analysed. How was such radical change possible in what seemed such a short period of time? Why were the pessimistic predictions of most political commentators proved wrong? What had happened to the right-wing forces who had been able to determine the outcome of critical national debates? How could a small, relatively powerless, community win its demands so effectively and comprehensively?

This pamphlet puts forward the idea that these changes stem from positive traditional Irish values arising from the anti-colonial struggle reinvigorated and amplified by the new social, cultural and economic influences of the 1960s onwards. Allied to these favourable social conditions were the reforming policies of the Fianna Fáil and Labour coalition and a Minister for Justice who was enthusiastic about introducing law reform. However, these reforms, both in their timing and quality, were not inevitable. The vital factor linking the favourable social conditions and the political decision to introduce equality legislation was the work of the lesbian and gay movement.

From the mid-seventies to his momentous victory in the European Court of Human Rights in 1988, David Norris doggedly continued his legal action to abolish the criminalisation of gay *sexuality*. Parallel to this legal action, the lesbian and gay movement established itself and slowly built up support, turning defeats into victories, developed its own political analysis and gained in confidence and experience. GLEN (Gay and Lesbian Equality Network) evolved from that movement and, in 1988, was given the remit to campaign for equality, a remit that was subsequently formalised into the twin aims of law reform on the basis of equality and anti-discrimination legislation for all disadvantaged groups. It was a deliberate decision to link sexual with social and economic demands and it was this link which helped to strengthen and inform much of the debate.

The perception of the Irish people as irredemiably 'backward' on sexual and social issues was an idea that GLEN refused to accept. While there are obvious contradictions in Irish attitudes, GLEN knew that there was a tradition of tolerance, which was benign, and based on a belief in fairness and justice. GLEN knew that there were real and positive traditional Irish values, arising from the struggle against colonialism and for civil, religious and economic rights, which could be activated, and the demand for equality was attuned to this heritage. Many of the lesbian and gay activists involved in GLEN were from the generation that had grown up in the 1960s, and they saw themselves as part of the profound changes which had taken place in Ireland since then but which had not yet been translated into legislative and institutional reform.

The evolution of lesbian and gay politics in Ireland emerged from a background of international developments and domestic change. The following chapters examine the beginning of contemporary lesbian and gay activism and the contributing factor that led to a development of a political consciousness. Chapter 2 looks at the international and historical background to the development of a lesbian and gay movement in Ireland. As the Irish lesbian and gay rights movement evolved, a large number of key social and political initiatives were taken, and these are examined in detail in Chapter 3. The difficult road to law reform is also described with an analysis of the opposition influences during that campaign in Chapter 4. Chapter 5 looks to the future and outlines the economic and social changes which are necessary to achieve equality, and goes on to examine the significant role Ireland could play in fostering the rights of lesbians and gay men internationally.

2 STONEWALL AND BEFORE

> It was a wonderful moment of explosive rage in which a few transvestites and young gay men of colour reshaped gay life forever. (John D'Emilio, 1992)

On Friday, 27 June 1969, around midnight, New York police raided the Stonewall Inn, a gay bar on Christopher Street in the heart of

Greenwich Village in New York. They expected it to be a routine raid but that night the gays fought back and the subsequent rioting continued for many hours. The image of drag queens rioting in the streets and engaging in combat with the helmeted officers of New York city's tactical police inverted the stereotype of gay men as meek, limp-wristed faeries. The street fighting and frivolity continued the following night and at one stage, riot police swinging their clubs dispersed an impromptu chorus line of gay men in mid-high kick (D'Emilio, 1983).

Stonewall happened at a time of great political ferment in the United States and it was not long after the riot that the mass movement, the Gay Liberation Front (GLF), was formed. The name adopted for the movement echoed that of the National Liberation Front in Vietnam, a signal that the GLF saw itself as part of a revolutionary process. The movement soon spread outside the US. The following year a GLF group was set up in London and subsequently in other countries in Europe, including Ireland. The GLF developed a basic analysis of gay 'oppression': it was not just a matter of prejudice or misinformation, which could be eradicated through education. In a manifesto they stated: 'We are a group of men and women formed with the realisation that complete sexual liberation for all people cannot come about unless existing social institutions are abolished.' They talked of liberation from oppression, resisting genocide, and making a revolution against 'imperialist Amerika'.

It can be argued that Stonewall and the emergence of the politics of the GLF created a new language for homosexuals. The emphasis was on pride and affirmation; these gay people were 'blatant, outrageous and flamboyant'. Discarding an identity conditioned by notions of sickness and sin, they represented homosexuality as a revolutionary path towards freedom. They engaged in public displays of affection and violated gender conventions. Sexual expression was seen as a form of personal, political action that was subversive, liberating and a way of building solidarity. 'Coming Out', the public affirmation of a gay identity, became a key political act. Another key concept was that of self-oppression, which according to a pamphlet of the time, *With Downcast Gays*, 'it summarised all that was important in gay liberation—the realisation that inasmuch we were agents of our own oppression, so we have the power to overcome it.' These gay liberationist values were to provide the ideological basis for the first generation of Irish gay activists.

ORIGINS

The emergence of the concept of homosexual rights has its origins in the late-nineteenth century with the first organised, self-conscious, collective resistance in Germany. Slowly but steadily this consciousness spread to Britain, the Netherlands and France. The late-nineteenth century also saw a deepening hostility towards homosexuality from what Lynne Segal (1990) has described as 'the late-Victorian storm-troopers of a new aggressive masculinity', which she links with the British imperialist expansion of the time. In explaining the homosexual purges of the 1880s, and the 1885 legislation which criminalised all sexual intimacy between men, Jeffrey Weeks (1977) states that: 'The year 1885 was one in which imperialism and national decline were on everybody's mind. The issue of Home Rule for Ireland and the threat of the break-up of the United Kingdom were looming.'

The Irish nationalist press pursued 'homosexual scandals' from the opposite direction, as a means of undermining certain highly-placed officials in the colonial administration in Dublin, one of whom was said to bear 'the odium of contaminating the running stream of Irish moral purity by stirring up the stink of pollution planted by foreign hands' (Breen, 1990). It is significant that Irish nationalist ideology developed during such a homophobic period in European history.

The homosexual movement is often closely associated with the socialist movement during the 1890s and early 1900s, when a good deal of discussion about sexuality, family and alternative ways of living took place. Oscar Wilde's radical politics are evident in *The Soul of Man Under Socialism* in which he envisioned the opportunities socialism would present for human culture. The pamphlet gained a reputation amongst oppressed people, according to Wilde's friend and biographer, Robert Sherard, and millions of copies were sold in Europe and America. In 1895 when Oscar Wilde was on trial, Edward Bernstein wrote a detailed defense of it which was published in *Die Neue Zeit*, the most prestigious journal of the Second International. In the early 1970s this was still regarded as 'one of the best and most advanced expositions on the subject of homosexuality to come out of the socialist movement' (Lauristen and Thorstad, 1974). The rise of fascism and Stalinism led to a decline in the movement for sex reforms. According to Sheila Rowbotham (1977), the rise of the new socialist orthodoxy within the revolutionary movements led to the dismissal of the political significance of sexual and personal politics, and 'was part of and contributed towards the theoretical and practical stunting of revolutionary politics.'

The Nazi persecution of homosexuals had up until Stonewall received little serious attention from historians. Since then much historical research has described and analysed the Nazis' violent paranoia about homosexuality. They were keenly aware, indeed paranoid, that their glorification of the male fighter could encourage homosexual desire, and 'once rife', according to Adolf Hitler, 'it extends its contagious effects . . . to the best and most manly of characters'. This focus on fear of homosexual desire itself is seen clearly in the 1935 law, which criminalised homosexual kisses, embraces, glances, and even fantasies. The homosexuals who were rounded up and sent to the concentration camps were forced to wear a pink triangle on their prison clothes. They were usually near the bottom of the prison hierarchy, and were often singled out for special tortures and dangerous work. After the 'liberation', many were not released because they had been 'legally' sentenced for criminal offences which still existed—they were not considered to have been unjustly imprisoned and so they were not entitled to compensation. The pink triangle became a symbol of resistance and pride for the new gay movement, and the collective memory of the horror of the camps was kept alive, for example, with plays such as *Bent*. Later, AIDS activists were to renew the meaning of the pink triangle with the added slogan SILENCE = DEATH.

Political action by homosexuals began afresh after the war in countries such as the US, the Netherlands and Denmark. However in the US during the 1950s there were determined campaigns against political and sexual dissidents: 'Sexual perverts . . . have infiltrated our Government in recent years' warned the Republican Party national chairman and they were 'perhaps as dangerous as the actual Communists'. Many of the gay activists were of course a combination of horrors, being socialists or communists as well. It is believed that in the McCarthy era, more people lost their jobs for being homosexual than for being communists (D'Emilio, 1983).

There has been little research into Irish lesbian and gay history before the 1970s, but even though our knowledge is fragmentary, it is clear that there are numerous sources awaiting researchers with relevant questions. The Brehon Laws regarded 'homosexuality' non-judgementally as one of the reasons for divorce. Early and medieval Irish poetry is frequently homoerotic, and the pre-Famine era is generally accepted to have had a more open attitude towards sexuality. It is ironic but important to note that, while homophobia can be regarded as part of the colonial inheritance, the nationalist press pursued homosexual scandals amongst highly placed officials with great vigour. The aim was obviously to discredit the British administration in Dublin, but it does illustrate that there was an organised sub-culture in the city, at least from the latter part of the nineteenth century. According to a Government Committee in the

1930s, 'gross indecency between male persons' was 'spreading with malign vigour', due in part, they believed, to lack of parental control and responsibility during a period of general upheaval, and the proliferation of places of popular amusement such as dance-halls, picture houses and motor cars. In 1946, a Labour Party report on Portlaoise prison stated that 'homosexuals constituting 30 per cent of the total are kept apart from other prisoners'.

The evidence we do have for the existence of lesbian and gay lives in Ireland, therefore, comes from those who were seeking to *control* homosexuality: no direct evidence–such as memoirs or diaries–from lesbians and gay men has yet been uncovered. The lives of writers and revolutionaries do however feature prominently: Oscar Wilde, Roger Casement, Pádraig Pearse, Eva Goore-Booth, Sommerville and Ross, Forrest Reid, Kate O'Brien, Brendan Behan and others. Indeed recalling Yeats's lines 'the ghost of Roger Casement is beating on the door', it seems that homosexuality haunts Irish history and culture. The history of homosexuality in Ireland has yet to be written, but there is no doubt that it will enhance our understanding of Ireland's varied communities just as women's history and labour history have already added new dimensions to our understanding of Irish identity.

3. Twenty Years a Growing

Few societies have changed so rapidly and so radically as has the Republic of Ireland since 1960. (Breen et al, 1990)

What may have seemed like a rapid change in the status of gay people in Irish society was in fact the result of a twenty-year campaign on many fronts. While the high profile example of the gay activists in the US and Britain provided the necessary impetus, it was the fundamental economic and social changes that had taken place in Ireland since the 1960s that allowed social movements such as the lesbian and gay movement to establish themselves. While the rest of western Europe boomed in the post-war period and implemented basic Welfare State principles, Ireland stagnated in isolation, unable or unwilling to tackle its considerable economic and social problems.[1]

Eventually the crisis in the late-1950s led to an unprecedented state intervention in the economy, the abandonment of protectionism, and the opening up of the economy to foreign investment. There was a huge increase in GNP, the numbers of skilled manual and white collar workers rose dramatically and emigration fell until there was net immigration in the 1970s. The pre-1960 agrarian economy's need for sexual repression (of heterosexuals at least) – uniquely few and late marriages, low birth rates outside marriage and lack of contraception–had changed fundamentally. There also followed a series of social initiatives such as free second-level education and grants for third-level education. Telefís Éireann was established in the early 1960s and censorship was relaxed. Various progressive movements were established, such as the Irish Family Planning Association in 1969. There was increased labour and left-wing militancy, especially with the setting up of the Northern Ireland Civil Rights Association. Staff associations such as the Local Government Official Union were developed into strong unions through the establishment of substantial strike funds. For lesbians and gay men, this new union, the Local Government and Public Services Union (LGPSU) and the people who built it, were to be enormously influential in the years ahead.

The second wave of the women's movement in Ireland began with the founding of the Irish Womens Liberation Movement in 1970. 'The sacred cows of social and political life in Ireland were quickly under attack from this small group of women', wrote Ailbhe Smyth in 1988. The IWLM caught the attention of the media as no group of Irish women had ever done, 'shocking, controversial, galvanising substantial numbers of women to take action . . . on a whole range of new issues'. It was particularly the women's movement, in combination with these changes in Irish socio-political culture, that created the space in which a gay movement could form.

THE IRISH GAY RIGHTS MOVEMENT (IGRM)

The 1970s was the time when the gay movement established itself, and began work on many issues, some of which are still with us today. The Irish Gay Rights Movement (IGRM) was founded in 1974 in a blaze of energy and optimism, when radical change seemed possible, necessary and immediate. The IGRM set up a Gay Centre in a fine Georgian building in Parnell Square in Dublin, which housed a disco, social room, offices, telephone line and a library. If Stonewall was an attempt to defend a space for gay people to socialise, the establishment of the IGRM was, to a great extent, an attempt to create that space. Twenty years later these basic facilities, where lesbians and gay men can meet, make friends, flirt, fall in love, are still woefully inadequate and virtually absent outside Cork, Dublin and Belfast.

Another priority for the IGRM was to neutralise Ireland's anti-gay laws. They achieved this by successfully supporting defendants so that, according to David Norris, 'within a few years the numbers of arrests by young police officers anxious to accumulate a high score of convictions had dropped to virtually nil'. This *de facto* law reform was a major achievement for the fledgling gay movement. However, in the Seanad debates on the Law Reform Bill, David Norris recalled 'the humiliation caused to those accused even when we secured their acquittal.' The seventies also saw the first pickets—outside the Department of Justice and the British Embassy—and the first gay pride demonstrations. There was widespread media coverage but in 1976 the RTE Complaints Advisory Committee ruled that a programme on homosexuality, which included an interview with David Norris, broke their broadcasting code as it did not reflect social mores. Publications such as *Gay News* and *Spare Rib* were also banned. There was a public furore over the refusal by Dublin Corporation to renew its grant to the Projects Arts Centre because it hosted the London theatre group, Gay Sweatshop. The controversy itself became theatrical with a Fianna Fáil Councillor on the Corporation Cultural Committee describing Gay Sweatshop as 'a crowd of nancy-boys from across the water'.

LESBIAN ORGANISATION

Lesbian action in Ireland has taken place to a great extent within the broad women's movement as well as separately, and at times with gay men. In 1975 Irishwomen United (IU) was formed and while it was primarily concerned with equal pay, contraception and violence against women, it did set out in its charter a demand for 'the right of all women to a self-determined sexuality'. While many of the women in IU were lesbians and had a high profile and a huge influence on the group, there was no public political activity around lesbian issues. Feminists were already breaking taboos by demanding free, legal, safe contraception, thereby admitting that they engaged in heterosexual sex. To admit publicly to lesbianism was unthinkable. Joni Crone a contemporary activist remembers that: 'We campaigned willingly and enthusiastically for the rights of our straight sisters. The idea of campaigning for our own rights didn't enter our heads until several years later when the first lesbian liberation group was formed.'

Nevertheless, IU was a place where lesbians felt free to express their views openly, and when it folded, many of the most active lesbian feminists emigrated to England. The same seems to be true in the North where lesbians formed the backbone of many groups and campaigns, although a lesbian group, Sappho, was established there in 1974. In 1978 a lesbian conference was organised in

Dublin out of which Liberation for Irish Lesbians was formed. For the next seven years, this group ran a telephone line, a women's disco and a discussion group. Joni Crone made a high profile debut as Ireland's first televised lesbian on the *Late Late Show* in 1980, and Liz Noonan ran as an independent lesbian feminist candidate in a Dublin constituency in the 1981 and 1982 general elections, receiving a good deal of publicity and a respectable vote.

NORTHERN IRELAND AND KINCORA

Writing in 1914, the Irish Socialist leader James Connolly predicted that if the country was partitioned there would be 'a carnival of reaction north and south', with the working class divided, and reactionary elements in control on both sides of the border. Up to recently this seemed an entirely accurate prediction with the North previously being slightly more liberal than the Republic because of the overriding influence of the London government. However, on the lesbian and gay issue, the North has been particularly and actively repressive, partly due to loyalists such as the Democratic Unionist Party (DUP), who have promoted a particularly virulent form of homophobia. There is also little doubt that the ongoing war has left little space for social movements such as the lesbian and gay movement to develop. The Catholic middle class in the North are more likely than their counterparts in the south to look to the Church for support and to heed its advice, as evidenced by the recent votes of the Social Democratic and Labour Party (SDLP) MPs in Westminister against a proposal to provide for an equal age of consent for gay men. Nevertheless, while recognising that there are particular problems in Northern Ireland, it would be unfair and counter-productive to stigmatise the people of that area as being inherently anti-gay.

The only example we have in Ireland of a moral panic directed against homosexuals is the Kincora affair in Northern Ireland, where there was a concerted attempt by a health board to identify and sack all youth workers who were lesbian or gay. This witch-hunt arose in connection with a confused scandal of sexual abuse in an adolescent Boys' Home. *The Irish Independent* broke the story in January 1980 and alleged that there was a cover up by both police and the social services department. There were also allegations that MI5 were involved in order to collect information as part of a 'dirty tricks' operation to discredit particular politicians when they were endangering British security interests. Some media reporting at the time was quite negative and tended to link homosexuality with sexual exploitation and abuse of young people. The sociologist Marie Smyth (1990, 1991), who researched the controversy, notes that this led to a 'discernible growth in homophobia'.

An official report in June 1982 by a social worker from the Department of Health and Social Security (DHSS) in London recommended increased monitoring of Children's Homes, more staff training and the introduction of a complaints procedure for residents. However, these recommendations were ignored. In January 1984, another inquiry was set up under Judge William Hughes. In spite of evidence to the contrary, the scope of the inquiry was narrowed to consider only homosexual abuse—heterosexual abuse of children was not examined. In December 1985, the Hughes inquiry was published; it made fifty-six recommendations, including a recommendation that the DHSS establish the legality of excluding homosexuals from employment in residential child care. The attempt to fire all lesbian and gay workers connected with child care was resolutely opposed by the trade unions and finally the London government forced the local health board to call a halt to its purge.

In explaining Kincora, Smyth argues that the moral panic analysis is insufficient and that issues of gender and the politics of Northern Ireland must also be examined. Kincora was an almost exclusively male institution where masculinity was prioritised and 'In such a milieu, victimisation is tolerated and even encouraged and complaints are seen as a sign of weakness.' William McGrath, one of those convicted of abuse, was a fairly prominent member of the Orange Order and had founded his own loyalist paramilitary group, Tara. The loyalists at that time were engaged in a 'Save Ulster from Sodomy' campaign to ensure that homosexuality was not decriminalised. He was a disciplinarian in the Boys' Home and maintained a strict regime, but he also surpassed the others in the brutality and ruthlessness of his abuse. According to Smyth, 'McGrath embodies some of the sexual and political contradictions of religious and political fundamentalism.' As the evidence emerged, it became clear that children and young people in Kincora had been systematically abused over a twenty-year period whilst in the care of the State and it also became clear that the interests of the victims were subverted to the larger interests of the security services, the State and loyalist political parties.

The Collectives

Within a few years of its founding, the IGRM split for reasons that seemed mostly to do with personalities but there also seemed to be differences over the importance that should be placed on the legal action in pursuit of law reform. Whatever the reasons for the split, it resulted in considerable squabbling, a duplication of effort and a waste of very scarce resources. One of the results of the split was that a group of mostly left-wing gay men in Cork decided in 1980 to set up an independent organisation, the Cork Gay Collective. The Collective was a motley crew and included a returned emigrant, an Australian, a County Council official, the President of the Students Union, an ex-hippy and, from time to time, a priest. We were regarded as a threat by the Cork-based IGRM and were reduced to holding our meetings in the dingy and draughty upstairs room of a pub. However, for all that, the Collective and its later counterpart in Dublin, both in their politics and in their non-hierarchical structure, were to be at the cutting edge of gay political action in the 1980s.

In 1981 and very much in the spirit of the time, the Collective adopted a manifesto, which encouraged gay people 'to have a positive view of their sexuality, to live fully and to challenge society's control by coming out in the family, work, church and social life'. Seeing the repeal of the anti-gay laws as merely the beginning, the manifesto called for equality in terms of jobs and accommodation, for freedom from harassment, for the equal right to express our feelings, and for positive information about sexuality. The Collective was 'convinced that this struggle cannot take place in isolation and that gay liberation involves the freeing of all oppressed groups'. The Collective would work towards forging links with other movements for social progress, in particular the women's movement 'recognising that our shared oppression derives from the abuse of sexuality as a tool of oppression which necessitated strict gender stereotyping and the denial of sexual fulfilment'. In a phrase redolent of that optimistic time, the manifesto declared 'further, we are internationalist and we pledge our solidarity with our sisters and brothers everywhere who suffer oppression because of their sexual orientation and we make this solidarity part of our practical work'. It concluded with the statement that 'we are products of society's conditioning and are aware of the danger of oppressive relations among ourselves'.

FIRST NATIONAL GAY CONFERENCE

The Collective initiated the First National Gay Conference, which was held in 1981 in Connolly Hall, an impressive trade union building in Cork. The conference was an ambitious undertaking with about 200 people attending plenary sessions, workshops, cinema and video screenings, a bookshop and exhibitions and finishing with a gala ball. The theme of the Conference was 'Gays in the 80s–Which Way Forward?' and was a response to 'an accepted need for a general assessment of the progress of the gay movement in Ireland to date and to consider fresh initiatives for the future'. The work of the conference was carried out in plenary sessions and in eighteen workshops on various topics, which included gay identity, disabled gays and gays and the women's movement. A total of forty-nine motions were passed and these set the agenda for the lesbian and gay movement for more than a decade. The conference made a significant contribution to the development of an indigenous theory and practice of lesbian and gay politics in Ireland.

The conference called for equality in the criminal law and for anti-discrimination legislation as well as for more support for lesbians and the women's movement in general. The conference also recognised the need for an autonomous gay activists group. The H-Block Hunger Strikes were ongoing at the time and three motions relating to the Republican prisoners' demands for political status and the 'national struggle' provided the only contentious debate. Another controversy took place in the newsroom of the *Cork Examiner* where journalists were not allowed to cover the conference, unlike all the other dailies, who gave extensive coverage to the event. Eventually the *Examiner* relaxed a little, and on the Monday, there was a very brief item headed 'National Gay Conference Concludes'.

Friends of ours from Britain and especially London made a significant contribution to the conference and the policies it developed. Two particular contributions stand out—Barry Prothero from the London-based National Council for Civil Liberties, warned that their 1967 law reform was a failure and that convictions of gay men had increased significantly afterwards. The other was the Gay Rights at Work group, who had done very effective work in the British trade union movement and who became a model for our trade union activity. Various initiatives of the Greater London Council, such as 'Changing The World: A London Charter for Gay and Lesbian Rights', also had a strong impact both in their analysis and their sense of confidence.

The Quay Co-op

The establishment of a resource centre was an original objective of the Collective and we were centrally involved in setting up the Quay Co-op in Cork, a workers' cooperative including a bookshop, café, women's place and a resource centre, which opened in May 1982. The facilities made available and the paid jobs in the Co-op allowed Cork to become a powerhouse of initiatives and a confident example for the rest of the country. These initiatives have included the trade union network, Gay Health Action, the Irish Quilt Tour of 1991 and the Lesbian and Gay Film Festival. The Cork experience shows that with resources and expertise, it is possible to build up a supportive community that can dramatically improve the quality of people's lives and which can, in turn, achieve progressive change in the wider community.

The Abortion Amendment Campaign was ongoing at the time and gay men were to become a driving-force in the campaign giving it a sense of energy and confidence. In many ways the 'right-to-life' amendment to the constitution was, in the short and medium term, a successful counter-attack by the Right against the gains made in the 70s but it also provided us with the opportunity to challenge conservative hegemony especially in what was a tightly knit town such as Cork. It allowed us for example, with some trepidation, to leaflet outside Masses against the amendment while priests inside preached for the amendment. While the campaign continued over more than a year and monopolised our attention, it also provided us with considerable skills, experience and confidence. The intensive local campaign resulted in the Cork City constituencies being unique in the country in having an anti-amendment vote higher than a pro-divorce vote of 1986.

Police Harassment and the Growth of Direct Action

Meanwhile in Dublin, a militant and radical group, later to be known as the Dublin Lesbian and Gay Men's Collectives, was established. One of the first actions of this group was to mount a defence campaign against harassment of gay men by gardaí who were supposedly investigating the murder of Charles Self, a gay man stabbed to death in his home in Dublin in January 1982. The investigation led to almost 1,500 gay men being questioned, photographed and fingerprinted at Pearse Street Garda Station. Many of the questions had nothing to do with the murder, but with the private lives of those being questioned. They were asked who they slept with, names and addresses of their gay friends and even what they did in bed. It became clear that the investigation was more concerned with compiling dossiers on gay men than it was with solving the murder. Many people were threatened that if they did not go voluntarily to the police station, the guards would turn up at their homes or at their workplaces, with devastating results for those who were not 'out'.

The murder was a particularly brutal one but the fear in the gay community was not of a murderer on the loose but of police intimidation. The Gay Defence Committee distributed a leaflet outlining the excesses of the gardaí and basic civil rights for individuals; a public meeting was held, and support was won from the Irish Council for Civil Liberties, the Prisoners' Rights Organisation and women's groups. Perhaps most significantly in terms of the community's confidence to defend itself, the battle was taken to the doors of the persecutors and a series of pickets were placed on Pearse Street Garda Station. This action generated widespread coverage in the media, and the interrogations stopped. While there were some problems relating to the investigation of a murder in Limerick in recent years, there has, in general, been little organised harassment of the gay community by the gardaí since.

Again, the situation for gay men in Northern Ireland is significantly worse, with the Royal Ulster Constabulary (RUC)

19

engaging in regular harassment of gay men. Writing to the Minister for Justice urging her not to introduce a British-style law reform, Jeff Dudgeon, who took the Northern Ireland case to the European Court of Human Rights, stated that the law is frequently used 'in an inhumane and cruel fashion, for no useful purpose'. Even during the last six years, there has been a series of local roundups of gay men in different towns, numbering up to twenty gay men and almost always involving a suicide because of the public disgrace and local exposure. The cases are invariably concerned with sexual activity in public areas such as parks or forests and have no under-age or coercive aspect. They frequently start, not because of a complaint, but because of a local police superintendent's prejudices.

In August 1982, a young man was walking through Fairview Park, a known cruising area for gay men on Dublin's northside. A gang of youths chased him, caught him and beat him to death. In 1983, these men were given suspended sentences and set free immediately having been found guilty of the killing. The gang held a 'victory march' in Fairview Park shouting 'we are the champions'. Previously, one of the gang had told the gardaí that 'a few of us had been queer-bashing for about six weeks before and had battered about twenty steamers'. This lenient treatment, together with the comments of the trial judge, led to a public outcry. The response instigated by the Dublin Gay Collective was a classic of radical leadership at a moment of crisis and a pivotal event in the evolution of the lesbian and gay movement in Ireland. The Collective won the argument that a protest march was essential and that it had to be out from the city centre to the Park and through the area where the killers lived. It was to be a defiant public statement that gay people would not be frightened off the streets and out of public places.

It was also argued successfully that it should not be a protest demanding longer prison terms but one against violence and partic-ularly against the judgement, which was seen to encourage and condone attacks on anyone thought to be gay. The banner leading the march had the simple message 'Stop Violence against Gays and Women'. The march was supported by a wide range of women's, students', trade union, progressive, and anti-amendment groups, reflecting the links built up in the course of the then current abortion amendment campaign.

THE MID-EIGHTIES AND THE DECLINE OF ACTIVISM

By the mid-eighties the litany of defeats for the left and liberals was alarming, and included the abortion and divorce referendums, the repressive Criminal Justice Bill, the banning of abortion information and the victimisation of women in many high-profile cases as well as soaring unemployment and emigration. Joe Lee describes the country at that time as 'stumbling towards the future with tragedy in the North and gloom in the South'. Writing in 1988, Ailbhe Smyth suggests that women's new found confidence and energy was 'well nigh quenched by the fundamentalist repression and the economic recession'. The lesbian and gay movement was also in retreat and in 1985, Liberation for Irish Lesbians was dissolved, the national gay conferences and the pride marches ceased and the Hirschfeld (gay) Centre burnt down. The Collective in Cork was reduced to a core of about four of the original members, as numerous gay men got involved for a short time and then emigrated. The Dublin Lesbian and Gay Mens Collectives stopped meeting around the time of the publication of their groundbreaking book *Out for Ourselves: The Lives of Irish Lesbians and Gay Men*. The book was the first to deal openly with lesbian and gay experience in Ireland but was ignored by the media, and both the Sinn Féin and Workers Party bookshops refused to stock it. These were not times for militant activism on the streets but for small task-orientated groups dealing with a specific issues, trying to rebuild confidence and laying the foundations for future progress.

21

The AIDS Crisis

As in so many countries throughout the world, it was left to the gay community to organise the first effective responses to the AIDS crisis and Ireland was no exception. Despite official unconcern, it was obvious to gay activists that Ireland would not escape the virus, and in January 1985, Gay Health Action (GHA) was founded with the support of a united gay community. It produced the first Irish AIDS information leaflet in May 1985, some weeks before it was confirmed that the virus was indeed established in the country. The print costs of the first 15,000 leaflets was met by the Health Education Bureau (HEB), but further funding was vetoed by the Department of Health because their legal advice was that information relating to gay sexual practices would be contrary to the criminal law. This was extreme duplicitousness as the Government was defending those very same laws in the European Court of Human Rights on the basis that they were not being implemented. While the Department of Health could not allow itself to support a gay mens health project the Department of Labour was, under trade union influence, funding a social employment scheme for Gay Health Action. The hostility of the Department of Health is evidenced by the refusal to meet with the GHA at any time under both Labour and Fianna Fáil ministers. This neglect was grossly irresponsible and almost certainly cost lives.

The failure of the Department of Health had two effects. The first, simply enough, was that GHA had to fund-raise for all the leaflets, posters, and safer-sex cards—nearly half a million items. For two years these formed the only available information on AIDS in the country, and were used way beyond the gay community: private fund-raising was, in effect, being organised in order to provide a basic public health service. A much more serious effect of the Department's neglect of the crisis is the ongoing refusal of the Government or any of its agencies to include relevant information on gay sex practices in its own campaigns. GHA could, by definition, reach only those men open enough to have some contact with the community. It could never reach those thousands of men who have sex with men yet who form no part of any gay community. For fear of embarrassment or censure, they were still ignored and were left open to a preventable, fatal, disease.

While the various statutory health bodies avoided their responsibilities, it was left to a small group of gay men and lesbians with few resources to keep up with international developments and disseminate this learning throughout the country. For at least two years the GHA was the only organisation providing information and advice to the gay community, to other 'at risk' groups, to professionals and to the media. GHA's work was described by Dr Derek Freedman in his book *AIDS—The Problem in Ireland* (1987):

> This group, on its own initiative and with little or no funding, set about informing people, organising lectures, producing leaflets, providing a telephone helpline service, and set up an HIV+ counselling group. This occurred years before anyone else saw the need. They have provided a caring service to the community at large, on a voluntary basis, and at no cost to the health services. They have been rewarded with an apparent low HIV rate and a REDUCTION in the rate of AIDS cases in the gay category since 1985.

GHA helped in the establishment of Cairde (a support and befriending group for those who are HIV+ or with AIDS), the AIDS helpline, and later the AIDS Alliances to coordinate the various projects. They also cooperated with lesbian workers within GHA to found Lesbian Health Action as a sister group. At an international level they helped to found the British–Irish network NOVOAH; and Chris Robson of GHA, a delegate to the first world NGO AIDS conference in Vienna in 1989, was centrally involved in the foundation of ICASO, the International Council for AIDS Service Organisations. He was also instrumental in setting up the European council and served on it for three years helping to develop its charter and formulate policy.

Another effect of the GHA was that it managed to challenge the initial, sometimes hysterical, anti-gay media coverage and develop a positive image of the role of the gay community as being responsible, effective and caring. Subsequent attempts by Family Solidarity to use AIDS as a stick with which to beat the gay community failed and indeed had the opposite effect of undermining their case.

Partly due to official neglect and hostility and partly due to the related exhaustion of the activists in GHA, it was decided to disband the group in 1990 and to allow its general work to be subsumed into the AIDS Alliance. It was hoped that another group would form and take over the role of GHA but unfortunately this did not happen. The rate of HIV transmission amongst gay men is no longer declining and may even be increasing, reflecting a worldwide trend. With the demise of GHA, there was no agreed and determined response from the gay community to the continuing AIDS crisis and, again reflecting a worldwide pattern, the needs of gay men, including the thousands who emigrate, were sidelined by both the voluntary and statutory sectors. There were sporadic initiatives such as the gay men's health project of the Eastern Health Board, the funding of a safer-sex leaflet by the Southern Health Board and the European Community funded conference on gay men's health organised by Aidswise in 1993. However none of these initiatives are enough to deal with the ongoing crisis, especially since recent scientific research, revealed at the Ninth International Conference on AIDS in Berlin in 1992, shows that the mechanisms HIV uses to destroy the body's immune system are far more complex than previously thought. These findings dim hopes that AIDS can soon be treated with a single 'magic bullet' drug or prevented with a vaccine. There is also the continuing problem of prejudice: the Irish

Medical Council guidelines suggest that it is acceptable to dis criminate against AIDS patients; in 1993 RTE refused Department of Health advertisements relating to condoms and referring to its Catholic ethos, the Mater Hospital banned certain information material on HIV prevention (RTE are now presenting comprehensive health advertising on the dangers of AIDS).

However, one of the positive effects of the law reform has been to release the energies of the gay community in a different direction and there is now a renewed commitment to tackle the HIV and AIDS crisis in a coordinated way. In addition we are now fortunate enough to have a Minister and a Department of Health who are committed to working in partnership with the gay community. There are now further possibilities for progress. (GLEN, 1994)

BUILDING ALLIANCES AND CONCENSUS

A significant number of lesbian and gay activists were also committed trade unionists and it is not surprising that they worked with in their unions for their rights as workers. In 1987 the Irish Congress of Trade Unions (ICTU) launched a radical and action-orientated policy document *Lesbian and Gay Rights in the Workplace: Guidelines for Negotiators*. This was the first detailed pro-gay policy from a powerful national organisation and it resulted in significant practical and ideological progress. The document quoted from the ICTU Women's Charter of 1985, which: 'recognises and demands the right of everyone, irrespective of sex, marital status or sexual preference to pursue their economic independence and to full participation in the social, cultural and political life of the community in conditions of freedom, dignity and equality.' 'Trade union policy on lesbian and gay rights', it stated, 'is an integral part of overall trade union policy to fight discrimination and protect workers' rights.' This was a response to a fairly common objection at the time that the rights of lesbians and gay men had little to do with the central task

25

of trade unions, which was wages and conditions of work. What these objectors in fact meant was that trade unions should only concern themselves with *their* interests, that is heterosexual and male workers.

The policy was comprehensive and dealt with all aspects of discrimination, including indirect discrimination in the workplace, the law, housing, harassment and violence and other areas. It recognised that harassment could arise from management or co-workers and that prejudice often focused on certain work areas, particularly those that involve young people. It called on unions to recognise that discrimination against lesbians and gay men is a trade union issue affecting thousands of workers and requiring a serious anti-discrimination policy and programme. It stated that underlying this discrimination is a pervasive heterosexism which is defined as 'the usually unquestioned consensus that lesbian/gay sexuality is unnatural and/or inferior to heterosexuality'. Detailed proposals for action were set out and they included a model agreement to be negotiated with employers. The ICTU also called for the repeal of the criminal laws and anti-discrimination legislation. This radical policy is unusual in international terms and has recently been used extensively in a European Union publication on harassment. The policy was the result of years of lobbying and was possible because of the space created for such policies by women and progressive trade unionists. By the 1980s the opposition to pro-gay motions at union conferences was usually muted and sometimes ideosyncratic.

In 1988, the Irish Council for Civil Liberties (ICCL) set up a working party, which included lesbians and gay men, to prepare a report—a combination of a 'research document and a practical, campaign orientated work'—to be known as *Equality Now for Lesbians and Gay Men*. The central part of the report was a detailed analysis and rejection of High Court and Supreme Court decisions which found that the anti-gay laws were not unconstitutional. The report set out in detail how the constitutional principles of equality, sexual privacy, intimate association and self-expression should be interpreted so as to guarantee the equal rights of lesbians and gay men. It argued strongly for equality in the criminal law and set out a model anti-discrimination Bill. Based on detailed research, it examined issues such as prejudice, homophobia, heterosexism, domestic partnerships, custody and adoption, employment, violence, education and young people, and freedom of expression.

The rigorous intellectual approach of the document made it invaluable for submissions to the Law Reform Commission, political parties and other organisations. Family Solidarity were to continually use its proposals as proof of our wider agenda, which it regarded as asking for 'revolutionary changes in the most fundamental values and institutions of our society'. In the classic New Right formulation of 'their' rights, these proposals 'would encroach on the rights and freedoms of those who reject the gay ideology'. (Using this formulation it could be argued that the abolition of apartheid encroaches on the rights and freedoms of racists.)

IMPACT OF THE NEW RIGHT

All through the twenty-year period, lesbians and gay men have had to fight against powerful heterosexist forces which were both traditional and modern and were vigorously renewed by the strident hostility of John Paul II's papacy and his appointees in Ireland. In 1990 Archbishop Connell of Dublin in a press interview described homosexuality as 'a disorder and an affliction'. The current papacy is actively homophobic. In one notorious 1986 encyclical the Vatican all but condoned anti-gay violence: 'When civil legislation is introduced to protect behaviour to which no one has any conceivable right, neither the Church nor society at large should be surprised when . . . irrational and violent reactions increase.' Another Vatican document of 1992 stated, 'The practice of homosexuality is seriously threatening the life and well-being of a great number of people.' Such is the threat represented by homosexuality, the document argues, that in certain cases 'it is not only legitimate but obligatory' to discriminate 'for example, in the assignation of children for adoption, in the hiring of sports coaches and in conscripting people into the military service'.

The Vatican document received widespread publicity and criticism in Ireland but were in the end ignored in practice as the government, employers and trade unions and others continued the work of introducing anti-discrimination measures. The policy was also criticised by a number of Catholic priests, one of whom wrote an article in the *Limerick Leader* headlined 'Why the church must reach out to the urban poor, the young, women and gay people'. Anti-gay attitudes are not exclusively Catholic. Ian Paisley is reported to have arrived to picket Belfast's Brook Clinic, a sexual advice centre for young people, 'bellowing' 'Lesbian Sodomites, Blasphemers, Haters of Christ, Haters of Morality . . .', at the counter-demonstrators (*IT* 28.1.93). In 1993 the new Moderator of the Presbyterian Church in Ireland said that the theme of his year in office would be a return to the basic teaching of the Church, including a return 'to the biblical teaching on homosexuality (let's not fudge this important issue by using this inept euphemism 'gay') . . . the tendency is itself not a sin—yielding to it is'.

In her book *Masterminds of the Right* Emily O'Reilly documents how a group of right-wing activists hijacked Ireland's social agenda for almost two decades. Their agenda was wide and included opposition to contraception, divorce, abortion, sex education, rape crisis centres, the 'stay safe' anti-abuse programme for schoolchildren, sexual advice for people with disabilities and of course the rights of lesbians and gay men. They were extraordinarily successful, especially in the 1980s, in winning two referendums, closing down the abortion referral services, banning all abortion information and in attaching a 'pro-life' protocol to the Maastricht Treaty.

Much of their activities were covert. A leading right-wing activist wrote in 1988 that members of the Knights of Columbanus occupy positions of influence in many walks of life and at the highest level. They are asked to be confidentially politically active:

> We also need to keep our eyes on hospital boards; ethics committees; school boards; parent's groups; the Virgin record store selling condoms to adolescents . . . sex education programmes; trying to keep the right government in power, or at least the one which is the lesser evil. . . . Such a network (of activists) if well motivated and highly confidential could do wonders quietly without coming out openly as Knights. An organisation or a group is never more powerful than when it influences events without itself being regarded as the initiator.

The minutes of one section of a Knights' meeting in Dublin in 1982 reads:

> Concern was expressed at the increase in the activities of homosexuals and it was suggested that perhaps the industrial, commercial and professional panel might look into this matter.

In 1991 the Dublin Grand Knight set up a special current affairs team which subsequently targeted a lesbian and gay radio programme produced by a community radio station.

The opposition became overt in 1990 with the publication by Family Solidarity of their report *The Homosexual Challenge: Analysis and Response*. This was a detailed and superficially reasonable document although an underlying hostility was revealed when it referred to the the gay community as 'engendering a pool of infection and disease'. (Interestingly, the report concentrated solely on gay men and did not even refer to lesbians.) We were, it suggested, a 'well-organised pressure group, following its own distinctive ideology and demanding radical and far reaching changes in Irish law and public policy'. It is obvious that Family Solidarity kept detailed records and were quite well informed on the history, policies and organisations of the gay movement. If no other book was available to an isolated young lesbian or gay man, *The Homosexual Challenge* would be of great value as it shows clearly that there is a vibrant and assertive community out there for them. With their detailed references to (outdated and discredited) research, Family Solidarity were clearly trying to repeat their success in the divorce campaign when they won the arguments on the social effects of divorce. However, on the issue of homosexual law reform they lost the argument, and in a series of articles and letters in *The Irish Times* in the summer and autumn of 1991, GLEN was effectively able to counter their arguments with more credible research findings and professional opinion. While the Church and lay right groups were not able to halt all change, they were able to delay law reform, AIDS initiatives, progress for young people and direct public funding for our community services. Their resistance consumed much of the scarce resources of the gay movement.

It can be argued that one of the decisive events in recent years in terms of society's perception of the lesbian and gay community was the broadcasting of Gay Byrne's *Late Late Show* debate on homosexuality in 1989. Broad public opinion towards the lesbian and gay community was and still is ambivalent: tolerant but unsure. The *Late Late Show* debate signified a decisive shift in public attitudes. In order to set up the debate, Gay Byrne invited representatives from the lesbian and gay community and lay right groups to debate the issue of homosexuality and the Irish State. The programme, watched by hundreds of thousands of people all over the country, as well as in Britain, succeeded, as it often does, in airing the thoughts of ordinary people about extraordinary issues. In this programme, the country saw the right-wing psyche exposed and fearful. By maintaining our belief in the progressiveness of Irish society, GLEN offered a confident and optimistic alternative.

ILGO, and the St Patrick's Day Parade

Discrimination and massive unemployment at home has meant that emigration is a constant drain on our communities. There are separate Irish lesbian and gay communities here, in London, New York and other international cities. There are no definite figures available but it seems that about half of the Irish lesbians and gay men who are 'out' are living outside the country. This forced emigration had resulted in a difficult relationship of guilt and resentment between the Irish at home and abroad, with a tendency to ignore one another. However this was to change radically in April 1990 when around twenty Irish lesbians and gay men in New York came together and set up the Irish Lesbian and Gay Organisation (ILGO) and decided to apply to take part in the city's St Patrick's Day Parade. The parade organisers, the Ancient Order of Hibernians (AOH), bolstered by the strongly anti-gay Archbishop of New York, Cardinal John O'Connor, refused to admit them on the grounds that the AOH is pledged to uphold the teachings of the Catholic Church, which regards the practice of homosexuality as sinful. [2]

A year of controversy followed and it received intense media coverage in the US, at home and worldwide. In many ways the whole drama is a microcosm of Irish history illuminating the negative and positive aspects of our traditions. In 1991, one vaguely liberal division of the AOH invited ILGO to join them on the parade with the strict proviso that they carried no identifying banners or signs. On the day, over 300 Irish gays and various supporters marched, accompanied by the city's first black mayor, David Dinkins. At various stages along the route, they were pelted with beer cans, booed and screamed at. While the Irish abroad have played an important role in building the labour movements and other progressive causes, there is also a disheartingly negative tradition. As Anne Maguire, a leader of ILGO remarked, 'Deep down, the AOH are people who can't stand living in New York. They can't stand the idea of living with Blacks and Mexicans and Filipinos and queers and all the other groups that make up New York.' The controversy and legal wrangles continued in the second year and for a while it seemed that the parade would have to be cancelled. It is ironic that the most bitter controversy involving Irish gays took place in New York. In a front page editorial headlined 'Save the Parade', the New York-based *Irish Voice* declared:

> With no sign of mediation on the horizon, forces have been unleashed that may not only seriously disrupt this years parade but may irreparably damage this great spectacle for many years to come. The New York St Patricks Day Parade is the largest parade of its kind in the world, and a showcase for the achievements of Irish Americans in this country. Now it is in mortal danger.

What was really in danger was the meaning and heritage of the Parade. What was at issue was who would define what it is to be Irish. The AOH were in effect saying that to be Irish was to be Catholic and heterosexual. In a powerful article in *The Irish Times* on the eve of the Parade, an Irish American historian, Walter J. Walsh stated:

> It is sad, true, and today ironic that the New York Citys St. Patricks Day Parade was born to combat exactly the kind of intolerance now on display. The parade grew in resistance to ethnic hostility against Irish immigrants. . . . For two centuries, the parade has made a resounding public statement to this city and to the entire world that, even in poverty and against adversity, an immigrant community can stand proud and defiant in its shared identity.

The AOH were now trying to capture that powerful common symbol of Irish American cultural identity and use it for their own ends, 'to humiliate and degrade Irish lesbians and gay men by excluding them from the annual celebration of their national and ethnic cultural identity'.

To provide moral support for those in New York, Cork lesbians and gay men applied to take part in their local 1992 parade; they were accepted and won the prize for the best new float. A spokesperson for the parade organisers was quoted: 'I suppose you could say we are fairly progressive down here in Cork. The Junior Chamber as the organisers of the parade recognise that this group are a part of our society and have as much right to march as anybody else.' For the Irish at home the extreme reaction of the AOH seemed strange and served to highlight and encourage the growing confidence of Irish society to accommodate difference. Nell McCafferty probably spoke for many when she sent a message of support to ILGO: 'Beloved sisters and brothers, sex in all its variety adds to the gaiety of nations. Today you add a sparkle to smiling Irish eyes.'

In 1993 and 1994 the controversy still continued in New York and more than 200 lesbians and gay men were arrested for defying a court order requiring them to stay off the streets during the parade. The controversy also spread to Boston but in San Francisco, lesbians and gay men were invited to lead the parade.

ÁRAS AN UACHTARÁN

By the early 1990s and after nearly twenty years of lesbian and gay community action there was a renewed sense of confidence and achievement with far more people involved in a widening range of initiatives. So it seemed entirely appropriate that President Mary Robinson should invite thirty-five representatives of the lesbian and gay community from all parts of the country, north and south, to Áras an Uachtarán in December 1992. It is difficult to describe

33

our experience that day; it was sunny, the President's welcome was warm and friendly, the occasion was informal, we were in high spirits as we wandered around the stately rooms and garden. It was an emotionally charged atmosphere: here was a President for whom we and almost every other Irish person held the deepest respect, and in effect she was saying to us 'You are fine people, I value your work and you are very welcome here.' It seemed to me that those years of struggle, exclusion and abuse were being put behind us. The significance of being welcomed into the symbolic home of all Irish people also had a very practical effect in terms of the law reform campaign. Mary Holland, writing in *The Irish Times,* described it thus: 'Not for the first time, our President, effortlessly and generously subversive of entrenched prejudice, has given a signal that cannot be ignored.'

4. LAW REFORM

Law is the hidden infrastructure which conditions our society and pervades almost every aspect of our lives.
(Senator Mary Robinson, 1987)

I

One of the immediate tasks of the gay movement was to repeal or neutralise those sections of the 1861 Offences Against the Persons Act and the 1885 Criminal Law Amendment Act which criminalised sexual relationships and indeed any physical intimacy between men.[3] One of the first acts of the 1917 Bolshevik Revolution had been the removal of laws criminalising homosexuality and abortion: Ireland's revolutionaries showed no such enthusiasm for radical sexual politics and the British statutes were carried over into the legislation of the new State. As Kevin O'Higgins boasted: 'We were probably the most conservative minded revolutionaries that ever put through a successful revolution.' In the aftermath of the Civil War, the Catholic Church and the new State formed a close alliance to forestall political and moral chaos as they saw it.

While significant social reforms, such as employment equality legislation, were introduced in the 1970s, it was still difficult enough to get a Bill to legalise contraception published, let alone a Bill to allow for homosexuality. In 1977, Dr Noel Browne was literally laughed out of the Dail when he asked the then Minister for Justice to reform the law. It became clear that a constitutional action was the only avenue possible for reform and it was on that basis that a plenary summons was issued in the High Court by Mary Robinson SC on behalf of her client David Norris on 21 November, 1977.[4]

The case was heard in July 1980 with numerous experts giving evidence in favour of the plaintiff. According to David Norris the intention in bringing the case was 'to end the conspiracy of silence' and in this the court case was an undoubted success. The silence was broken and for the first time some of the realities of life for gay people received widespread and detailed media coverage and its generally positive nature helped shape public opinion on the matter. The Government called no witnesses to back up its case but argued trenchantly that sexual relationships outside marriage were unacceptable and that the state should do all in its power to stop the spread of homosexuality.

In delivering his judgement in the High Court on 10 October, 1980 Mr Justice McWilliam seemed to accept most of the case made by David Norris; indeed he summarised it elegantly in seven points, including that there was a large gay population, that there was 'no foundation' for the common negative stereotypes and that the significant discrimination experienced by gay people was reinforced by the criminal laws. According to David Norris, they were convinced that they had won but 'at the last minute there was a swerve in the judgement' and the judge found against the plaintiff.

In a majority 3:2 judgement in April 1983, the Supreme Court also found that the laws did not contravene the Constitution having regard to the Christian nature of the State, the immorality of the deliberate practice of homosexuality, the damage that such practices causes to the health of citizens and the potential harm to the institution of marriage. We were not surprised by the decision but were stunned by the approach and reasons given. In delivering the majority judgement, the Chief Justice began by stating that there were 'a large number of people in this country with homosexual tendencies', and that after decriminalisation, the small number of people who were exclusively homosexual would entice this larger group into 'more and more deviant sexual acts to such an extent that such involvement may become habitual'. So, many more people, in the view of the Chief Justice, would have, as a result, to endure the 'sad, lonely and harrowing life' of the exclusively homosexual man.

According to the ICCL, the majority decision 'was less an instance of impartial decision-making and more a case of law-making by prejudice'. Dissenting judgements were given by Mr Justice McCarthy and Mr Justice Henchy based on the right to privacy and the fact that the laws had already been ruled against by the European Court of Human Rights in the Dudgeon case in 1981. The ICCL publication *Equality Now for Lesbians and Gay Men* deals extensively and devastatingly with the majority judgements of the Irish courts. It refers to the dissenting judgements of Henchy and McCarthy as standing 'like beacons in a dark night'. Their judgements contain *inter alia* a forceful critique of interpretations of law and evidence composing the majority's judgement. The State submitted no expert evidence to rebut that submitted on behalf of the plaintiff and Justice Henchy observed that accordingly in an adverserial system 'the trial judge was bound in law to reject the Attorney General's defence and to uphold, at least in part, the plaintiff's case'. According to the ICCL, the basis of the dissenting judgements was that the rights claimed by the plaintiff were inherent in a free and equal human personality.

The decisions of the courts in the Norris case represent a failure of nerve to make the imaginative leap beyond prejudice and to put the rights inherent in the Constitution into effect. Since the mid-1960s, the Irish courts, prehaps influenced by the US Supreme Court, had issued judgements activating various personal rights inherent in the Constitution, including the right to bodily integrity, the right to work and earn a livelihood and the right to have access to the courts. In the McGee case in 1974 the Supreme Court established a right to privacy and struck down the laws which prohibited the importation and sale of contraceptives. According to the ICCL, the judges in the Norris case missed the point that at the heart of the privacy doctrine developed in *McGee* lies a right to freedom of sexual autonomy, intimate association and self-expression which cannot be stifled at the boundaries of formal marriage or procreational sex. The Irish courts were not unique in their prejudice. In 1986, the US Supreme Court made a similar decision in *Bowers v Hardwick*, stating that any claim that homosexual sodomy is protected by constitutional privacy is 'facetious at best'.

The Chief Justice underwent a change of opinion in the subsequent decade, claiming that the decision was widely misunderstood: 'It was taken as a decision by the court approving of the legislation criminalising homosexual acts. It was no such thing. In my judgment I said that I would probably be against a proposal to criminalise homosexual behaviour between consenting adults.' In an interview in *The Irish Times* in 1991, the Chief Justice said that in the 1937 Constitution, 'you find a whole Pauline tract, the whole Christian preamble. This is Dev's constitution. He'd be turning somersaults in his grave if he were told "Do you know that your constitution has been held to prohibit laws criminalising buggery?"' By 1991, the now-retired Chief Justice felt strongly that 'The Irish Government must change its domestic legislation. There is no constitutional bar. You just repeal it. It is not overturning our judgement.' However, according to one legal commentator at the time 'the fierce and colourful rhetoric' of the majority judges, which was unnecessary to their decision, made a law reform all the more difficult and was 'a dramatic rejection of its spirit'.[5]

II

It is a debilitating effect of Partition that gay men in a small island should have to undertake two separate law reform campaigns and take two cases to the European Court in order to establish their rights. However, both cases set the first legal precedents for the rights of gay men by the premier international human rights court. The Northern Ireland Gay Rights Association was set up in 1975 and immediately found itself embroiled in a police witch-hunt with twenty-three gay men being arrested.[6] The 1967 British law reform had not been transferred to Northern Ireland and the harassment galvanised the activists to challenge the anti-gay laws at the European Court of Human Rights with Jeff Dudgeon as plaintiff. In July 1977 the Northern Ireland Human Rights Commission recommended that the law be reformed and the Government announced that it would implement the recommendation. This prompted Ian Paisley and the Democratic Unionist Party to mount a 'Save Ulster from Sodomy' campaign. Two Unionist MPs led a caravan of more than sixty cars to Stormont to hand in their petition, which they claimed had been signed by more than 70,000 people. (Later, gay activists were to respond with a 'Save Sodomy from Ulster' campaign.) The law reform proposals were then shelved by both Labour and Tory governments who, according to Jeff Dudgeon, traded in 'pathetic little deals to sweeten both Paisley and the Official Unionists'.

The British Government also argued in Strasbourg that the opposition of the Unionists and the Catholic Church justified the refusal to reform the law. However, in 1981 the Court ruled that a total ban on homosexual conduct was contrary to the Convention on Human Rights. The Court did not accept the complaint against the discriminatory nature of the British 'reform' and stated that there could be criminal laws which would discriminate against homosexuality. The Catholic Church found itself in an unlikely alliance with Paisley's church and party as well as the Official Unionists and the Orange Order in opposing the London Government's law reform proposals. The law reform, based on the 1967 model, was passed by the House of Commons in October 1982. Gay people in the public gallery cheered and some were arrested.

Meanwhile, after the Supreme Court ruling, David Norris and his legal team, still including Mary Robinson at the time, continued their long, legal journeys to the European Commission on Human Rights. The Commission heard both David Norris and the Irish Government and then offered them an opportunity to settle the case at that stage. When they did not, the Commission itself made a ruling on the issue in favour of David Norris. As part of standard procedure, the then Fine Gael–Labour Coalition Government was given the opportunity of accepting this decision or contesting it before the Court. Following the Government's rejection of the Commission's ruling, the case was referred to the court in May 1987 and the hearing took place in April 1988. The Irish Government defended the case on the contradictory basis that the laws were not implemented but that they were necessary. It also argued that 'the moral fibre of a democratic nation is a matter for its own institutions and the Government should be allowed a degree of tolerance in their compliance' with the Convention. This can only be seen as a cynical exercise, as the decision in the Dudgeon case in 1981, in relation to Northern Ireland, set a clear precedent that the same total ban on homosexual acts was unacceptable. The Government for most of this period was a Fine Gael-Labour coalition with Garret Fitzgerald as Taoiseach, a politican who had launched a constitutional crusade to create a more pluralist Ireland.

On the 26 October 1988, the Court held by eight votes to six that the laws contravened Article 8 of the Convention on Human Rights.

The Irish representative was the Supreme Court judge Mr Justice Brian Walsh; he found against the plaintiffs in the Dudgeon and Norris cases. According to one commentator, his version of Lord Denning's 'appalling vista' appears to be 'the consensual moral conduct of persons un-versed in the precepts of natural law'. (*The Irish Times*, 25.4.92) The Fianna Fáil Government announced that it was considering the judgement, a process that was to continue for another five years.

Now that the law reform was a matter for the Oireachtas, it was time for a campaign by gay activists. As Ursula Barry has commented on the court actions with regard to both the campaigns for reproductive rights and homosexual law reform, 'those directly concerned and affected are reduced to spectators, watching experts slogging it out within the highly technical and formal atmosphere of the courts'. The previous September an open meeting of all lesbian and gay organisations and activists was held in order to prepare for the forthcoming campaign. It was agreed that our demands should be for equality in the criminal law and for anti-discrimination legislation. These were bold and radical demands, at a time when the Right seemed invincible. However, we were determined to win and we were not interested in moral victories. At the meeting, I said our task was to consolidate support around the principles of equality, to win over the doubtful, to pacify those oppressed and to isolate the bigots. A fundamental fear at this stage was that the Government would quickly introduce a law similar to the 1967 British 'reform'. This had copper-fastened the basic criminalisation of gay sexuality but allowed that sexual relationships between two men over twenty-one and in private would not be a prosecutable offence. 'In private' was so narrowly defined that a house in which a third person was present was excluded. Not surprisingly, this 'reform' had resulted in a quadrupling of convictions of gay men in that jurisdiction. Homosexuality within the armed forces and merchant marine remained illegal as did anal intercourse between heterosexuals.

As we already had a *de facto* law reform, our initial strategy was not to call for an early law reform but to build up a consensus that an equality-based law reform was the only option. The ICCL was still in the process of preparing its detailed policy document *Equality Now for Lesbians and Gay Men*, which was not to be published until 1990. Most importantly, the Law Reform Commission was still considering the matter and in 1989, in its Consultation Paper on Child Sexual Abuse, it recommended that 'with the possible exception of the age at which sexual autonomy should be allowed, the constraints imposed by the criminal law on consensual sexual activity should be the same for homosexuals as for heterosexuals.' Their provisional recommendation was for an equal age of consent of 17 years, stating that 'no case has been established for fixing a higher age of consent for homosexual activity'.

Submissions were invited and a seminar was held and attended by all the relevant professional and interest groups, including GLEN, Gay Health Action, the ICCL and Family Solidarity with the former groups arguing strongly that there had to be a common age of consent. There was little dissent from the provisional recommendations other than from those who objected to any decriminalisation of homosexual activity whatever. After this model process of policy development, the Commission published its Final Report in 1990 and recommended that the Victorian legislation be repealed and that there should be the same protection against both homosexual and heterosexual exploitation of the young, with an equal age of consent of seventeen years.

The Commission's recommendation was of the greatest importance because the rational argument for equality had been won at a mainstream and official level. Now it was not just the gay movement or civil liberties groups or the trade union movement who were arguing for equality but the government-appointed Law Reform Commission, which had carried out detailed research and consultation. As it turned out, it was one of the few LRC recommendations implemented. In a sense, it reflected what has been described as the 'objective secularisation' of Irish society that such an ideologically important agency should not have a clerical involvement and should be able to operate independently of Catholic theology. However, it may have been a matter of chance that other presidents of the LRC of a noted right-wing disposition on social and sexual issues were not in office at this critical time.

Our belief in the possibility of progressive law reforms received a great boost in November 1989 when the Government accepted amendments that homosexuals and Travellers should be given protection under the Prohibition of Incitement to Hatred Bill. The Government had previously argued against such amendments and it is said that as the new Minister for Justice, Mr Ray Burke, was about to speak, the Taoiseach, Charles Haughey, came into the chamber and spoke to the Minister, who then announced that the amendments were to be accepted. The Minister pointed out how important it was to protect homosexuals from campaigns of hatred at a time when they could be made the scapegoat for the frightening spread of AIDS. The Minister was showered with tributes from the opposition, according to newspaper reports. Another significant law reform the following year was the final and total abolition of the death penalty (not used since the 1950s), which received a wide welcome and almost no opposition. Using this reform as a model, I suggested that we should recall Willie Whitelaw's famous remark and 'go about the country stirring up apathy' about gay law reform. In April 1990, Dick Spring, leader of the Labour Party, launched the party's Equal Status Bill, stating that 'There is a fund of goodwill in Ireland towards the idea and principle of equality.' GLEN had a significant input to this Bill.

David Norris had been pressing for a debate in the Senate on the European Court judgement for some time and, spurred on no doubt by the election of Mary Robinson as President in November 1990, the Government allowed time for such a debate on the 12th of

December 1990. The Minister for Justice, Mr Ray Burke TD, set the tone for the subsequent contributions by stating that 'If we did not already have legislation which penalises homosexual acts in private between consenting male adults, I do not think that today any reasonable person could seriously argue for such legislation.' He then went on to outline the recommendations of the LRC and concluded by saying that 'I will listen with interest to these statements to hear suggestions as to what should be included in the forthcoming legislation.' Most important was the promise given by the Minister that 'I assure the House that as early as I can within a year, a gay law reform Bill will be introduced.' This was a promise to be repeated and broken many times in the next two years.

The debate that followed saw a general welcome for the recommendations of the LRC. The contributions were well-informed and thoughtful, with Senator David Norris making a particularly fine contribution and no doubt delighting in being able to address an Irish parliament on the issue after almost twenty years campaigning. Ireland had been remarkable in its ability to continually talk around sexuality in relation to contraception, abortion, homo-sexuality, sex education and divorce, while at the same time rarely talking about sexuality directly. Senator Brendan Ryan's contribution was an exception and dealt with sexuality in general, stating that 'it is actually very nice, very good, very self-affirming . . . It is not something dangerous to be allowed within carefully defined constraints for fear we would all go berserk if we were not carefully kept on a short leash.'

An important tactic throughout the campaign was to try to get people to look beyond Britain to the rest of Europe where most countries had laws based on equality. The Senate debate showed the effectiveness of this perspective and many senators spoke on this issue using the information we had supplied. Almost three years later Máire Geoghegan-Quinn defended her Bill by stating that 'if we could raise our sights beyond our nearest neighbour to the

European mainland we would realise that a common age of consent is the norm on the European mainland'. On 4 December 1990, the Dáil debated the Criminal Law (Rape Amendment) Bill. The Bill was widely welcomed for its progressive content, and unusually the Minister for Justice agreed to amendments from the opposition. The Bill was based on the recommendations of the LRC and the various offences of sexual assault, aggravated sexual assault and rape were defined in a gender-neutral way. This Bill was laying the foundations for an equality-based gay law reform by removing the need for different legislation for homosexual and heterosexual sexual assaults. In fact the Bill repealed that part of the 1861 legislation which related to indecent assault on a male person. Partly at the suggestion of GLEN, Pat McCartan TD of the then Workers Party proposed that the Bill delete all the relevant sections of the 1861 and 1885 legislation. Not surprisingly perhaps this simple solution to the law reform problem was not accepted by the Minister.[8]

In March 1991, the new Primate of All-Ireland, Cathal Daly, reiterated the uncompromising opposition of the hierarchy to any gay law reform, stating that it 'would not be genuine love towards people of this kind'. The Minister's promise to introduce a law reform within the year put the issue on the political agenda, and in June 1991 the Minister for State at the Department of Justice promised the Dáil that legislation would be introduced in the next session. Well-informed sources were telling us that there was very strong back-bench opposition to any reform and that we would be very naive if we were to believe these promises. We were of course a little naive but we were also continually building up support for the LRC recommendations and for our anti-discrimination proposals. The behind-the-scenes opposition and manoeuvring surfaced in September 1991 when the then Taoiseach Charles Haughey told the Dáil that the matter was still to be decided. Following lobbying by GLEN, the Progressive Democrats ensured that the revised Prog-ramme for Government of October 1991 stated that a reform would be introduced 'as speedily as possible'. The continuing strength of right-wing opposition within Fianna Fáil was made public when the chairman of the Fianna Fáil Parliamentary Party stated that he would continue his opposition despite the Programme commitment.

By this stage, GLEN had built up a wide concensus on the principle of equality and the need for anti-discrimination legislation including major organisations such as the ICTU, the National Youth Council of Ireland, the Council for the Status of Women, political parties and organisations representing people with disabilities, as well as Travelling community. The Church of Ireland also expressed its support for law reform and anti-discrimination legislation. Indeed the third anniversary of the European Court judgement provided the opportunity to launch such a broad-based 'Campaign for Equality'. Given this support and the continued prevarication of the Government, GLEN decided to concentrate on getting an early reform in the law. In November 1991 we lodged a complaint with the Council of Europe regarding the unacceptable delay in complying with the court judgement.

In February 1992 Charles Haughey finally stepped down as Taoiseach and Albert Reynolds was elected in his place. Almost immediately he was facing a crisis over what came to be known as the 'X case'. It was revealed that the Attorney General sought and was granted a High Court injunction on the basis of the 'right-to-life' amendment, preventing a fourteen-year old girl, a victim of sexual abuse, from travelling to Britain for an abortion. There was a public outcry and the Government encouraged the parents to appeal the decision to the Supreme Court, which was to decide that the right-to-life amendment to the Constitution allowed for abortion in certain circumstances. The Taoiseach was also under pressure from the opposition because of the Government's law reform commitment. He told the Dáil that 'no such legislation has been promised' only to have to retract the next day stating that 'yes, it is included in the Programme for Government'.

While the Government was prevaricating, it was also secretly promising the Council of Europe that legislation would be introduced speedily. The powers of the Council of Europe to secure the implementation of European Court of Human Rights rulings are cumbersome and ineffective when dealing with recalcitrant governments. The powers of the citizen are also limited and because the ECHR has not been incorporated into Irish law, it is not possible to take an action in the Irish courts. A citizen or group of citizens can take a case back to the ECHR to secure implementation of the original ruling and to seek damages but this is a lengthy and somewhat difficult and possibly expensive process. Nevertheless GLEN had received legal advice on the matter and was finalising such a case: this was never lodged because, happily, events made it redundant and politically inappropriate.

The member states of the Council of Europe oversee the implementation of the rulings of the ECHR and a defaulting state can be suspended or expelled from the Council for non-compliance. (Greece under the Colonels was the last State to suffer such a fate.) Effectively these issues were dealt with by the Committee of Ministers Deputies, civil servants at ambassadorial level, at six-monthly meetings. Again the role of the citizen or an Non Governmental Organisation (NGO) is extremely limited and the timing, agenda and content of these meetings are meant to be confidential. An NGO such as GLEN has no standing with the Committee and while it was informed of any submission we made, copies were not circulated. However, we were able to use our international contacts to lobby and keep other member states informed. Our efforts to get media coverage of the deliberations of the Committee were unsuccessful until shortly before the May 1992 meeting when a friend in the women's movement suggested we alert the Brussels correspondents of the Irish media. Committee sources revealed that the Irish representative, Ambassador Liam Rigney, had given a commitment that the Government would introduce legislation in 1992. In fact, the Ambassador was merely repeating the commitment which had been given six months previously when we had not been aware of just how valuable the Brussels correspondents could be.

This promise became a major news item and was covered extensively and prominently in all the newspapers, on RTE and independent radio. Sources within the Council were quoted as saying that there was increasing exasperation about Ireland's continuing failure to introduce legislation. The Government was thrown into confusion. It already had a major back-bench problem with the abortion issue being linked with the Maastricht Treaty on European Union. Now Family Solidarity were questioning whether the Norris case was 'another example of Europe imposing its ethical values on Ireland'.[9]

The Government were determined to get the Maastricht Treaty through in the referendum and a gay law reform was not going to be allowed to generate any greater opposition. The Taoiseach contradicted the Government's commitments to the Council of Europe, saying that 'the Ambassador was better informed than I am . . .I don't know where he got it. He didn't get it from Justice.' Two weeks later in the Dáil, he was to back-track again saying 'the Ambassador was following exactly the information available to him (from the Department of Justice) ... the Ambassador was quite in order in what he said'. Asked was he not concerned about the reaction of the Council of Europe, he indicated that he was not concerned and replied that such were the 'hazards of Government'. It should be said that the Taoiseach had written to GLEN on 7 May in a friendly and detailed manner and reaffirmed the Government's commitment to introduce legislation.

The pro-life campaigners mobilised their considerable resources to try to defeat the Maastricht Treaty in the referendum. According to newspaper reports at the time the assembled anti-abortion forces 'will also provide formidable opposition to any attempts at legalising divorce or homosexuality'. However, the Maastricht Treaty was passed by 69 per cent to 31 per cent of the votes cast. It was a serious set-back for the right-wing forces and they had used up a lot of their political capital especially in Fianna Fáil.

Later in the year, the Taoiseach was to say that law reform was at the 'bottom of the list of priorities'. This cavalier attitude to international human rights commitments seriously damaged the image of Albert Reynolds, and may have contributed to the mauling he received in the subsequent general election. However, he took a more liberal line when he indicated that on the continuing abortion issue there would be a strict separation of Church and State and he would not be consulting with the hierarchy or the pro-life movement for that matter. In addition he said that there would be no free vote for Fianna Fáil TDs on issues such as abortion, divorce and gay law reform.

By now the Taoiseach was being harried in the Dáil by all opposition parties, notably by Proinnsias de Rossa, leader of the Democratic Left, and Dick Spring, leader of the Labour Party. The delays were also creating tension within the Fianna Fáil–Progressive Democrat coalition with the PD chairman stating that there was no room for an 'à la carte' commitment to respect for human rights and international law. It was a low point for us but we saw little point in an angry demonstration and instead on the fourth anniversary of the European Court judgement we held a sardonic birthday party outside the Dail and announced that we were recommending that Ireland be suspended from the Council of Europe. The next meeting of the Committee of Ministers Deputies was held in early November 1992. Ambassador Rigney explained that the referendum on abortion and the preparation of the White Paper on divorce meant that it was not possible to address the homosexuality issue as well. In view of the forthcoming general election, Mr Rigney asked that the Government be given a further six months to comply with the judgement. While the Committee was known to be 'greatly disturbed' by Ireland's 'flagrant breach' of the Convention, a further six months were granted.

III

The General Election of November was a serious set-back for Fianna Fáil and particularly for Albert Reynolds. For Dick Spring and Labour, it was a major victory and they increased their seats from sixteen to thirty-three. During the campaign, they had given strong commitments to an immediate law reform and an Equal Status Bill. In abortion-related referendums held at the same time, amendments to ensure the right to information and the right to travel were passed by substantial majorities. A Government proposal to limit the right to abortion established by the Supreme Court was defeated by two to one.

Negotiations to form a new coalition government began and GLEN circulated a one-page document summarising its proposals. After some delay, Fianna Fáil and Labour entered into negotiations, and the 'liberal agenda' issues of divorce, gay law reform, contraception and abortion were given a high priority. According to one political commentator, the presidential reception for our community 'has strengthened the mood for change in this area'. Nevertheless gay law reform was to prove a sticking-point, and when finally the *Programme for Government* was published it included the familiar sounding commitment that legislation 'will be introduced in 1993 to bring our law into conformity with the ECHR'. The absence of the words gay or homosexual meant that it was unclear as to whether this commitment referred to the ruling on abortion information or gay law reform or both. What was to prove to be of the greatest importance was the priority given to a policy of equality: 'We are firmly committed to eliminating inequality for all groups in society that have suffered from disability, disadvantage or discrimination. A Cabinet minister will have responsibility for seeing that equality becomes a reality, through institutional, administrative and legal reform.' A commitment was also given to introduce equal status legislation which would prohibit discrimination on a wide range of grounds and would include sexual orientation and other categories. We were to highlight this commitment in the following months.

Máire Geoghegan-Quinn of Fianna Fáil was appointed Minister for Justice and Mervyn Taylor (Labour) was appointed as Minister for Equality and Law Reform. There was some confusion initially about who was responsible for law reform but it fell to the Minister for Justice. At our first meeting with the Minister for Equality we stressed that if one of the first pieces of government legislation was to copper-fasten inequality it would seriously undermine his commitment to equality in the Programme. Early on, the Minister for Justice indicated her enthusiasm for introducing a speedy law reform. In February, Ógra Fianna Fáil was given the go-ahead to publish its long delayed policy document on lesbian and gay rights, which strongly advocated the GLEN position. In March the Minister for Justice told the Ógra FF conference that she intended to introduce reform before the summer recess; she set out three options: to copy the British legislation, to restate the current law removing the more offensive wording in addition to removing the ban, or a thorough-going reform of the current law with completely new legislation. She welcomed the statement of the Minister for Defence that the defence forces should not be exempt from the law reform. She also set out three options concerning the age of consent, 17, 18 or 21 years and hinted strongly that 21 was unlikely. She also seemed to indicate that 18 as the age of majority would probably be more acceptable to the population at large. There were reports of disquiet amongst Fianna Fáil TDs such as the former Minister for Education, Noel Davern. Commentators reflected on the US 'gays in the military' furore and wondered whether the social agenda could be implemented. GLEN accepted, with some reservations, that the Government was intent on changing the law and began an intensive lobbying process to ensure that the reform would be on the basis of equality. A three-page briefing document was produced in February and published in an edited form at in *The Irish Times* the following month.

On International Women's Day, the Minister for Labour Affairs, Mary O'Rourke, published the Bill to amend the Unfair Dismissals Act and it included the provision that a dismissal on the grounds of sexual orientation would be automatically unfair. It would be difficult to overestimate the importance of this reform for workers who are lesbian and gay, and indeed, in order to stress its value to people's lives, GLEN consistently emphasised the practical importance of such an amendment to labour protection legislation by maintaining that it was as important as the law reform. In fact at times, GLEN was putting more painstaking effort into getting those two words 'sexual orientation' into that Act than it was into law reform. In many ways it was a classic piece of lobbying targeted at a major but achievable goal and identifying the precise amendment to be used, that is adding 'sexual orientation' to Section 6(2)(e) of the 1977 Act. The activists on this issue in GLEN had a trade-union background and no particular fondness for the Employers Federation. However, we realised that we needed their support or at least their acquiescence and so, because they were opposed to any extension of the powers of the Act, we sought their support on the basis that our proposal was a clarification of the terms of the Act. They replied fairly positively, stating that 'a dismissal for sexual orientation would be difficult to justify under existing law'. This law reform was particularly satisfying because it was an Irish initiative and was not a response to European demands. It was also a clear signal to us that the Government was serious about its equality commitments.

On 1 April GLEN met the Minister for Justice in Leinster House and this was to prove to be a very effective meeting. Most importantly, Phil Moore of Parents Enquiry, a group for the parents of lesbians and gay men, was part of the delegation and, as Chris

Robson, co-chairperson of GLEN, puts it, 'two Irish mothers met, took to each other and solved the problem between them'. The Minister was obviously well-informed on the issue and was well able to ask the difficult questions in relation to prostitution and sex in public, which we replied to on the basis that there should be no distinction between homosexuality and heterosexuality.

On April 22nd, our hopes were to be shaken when *The Irish Times* published a story based on a leaked copy of a draft memo to the Government on decriminalisation. The memo, which gave every indication of having been written by department officials at some previous date, set out two basic options regarding the law reform:

> The first option is to make the minimum change needed to satisfy the EC judgement. . . . It would leave the existing Sections 61 and 62 of the 1861 Act and Section 11 of the 1885 Act in place together with the common law offence of buggery but exempt from their effects, acts in private of buggery between consenting adults and of gross indecency between consenting male adults.

The memo went on to note that this was the approach adopted by Britain, 'As it leaves in place the existing provisions while providing for exemptions . . . *it retains the principle in law that the sexual conduct in question is unacceptable*' [*my italics*]. The second option was generally on the lines of the LRC recommendations with the repeal of the relevant sections of the 1861 and 1885 Acts and the common law offence of buggery. In fact it was the Department of Justice that recognised that full decriminalisation required the repeal of the common law offence, as the 1861 Act merely provided for penalties. An equal age of consent would be introduced, and Section 18 of the Criminal Law Amendment Act 1935 and the common law would deal with public acts of gross indecency.

The memo stated that this was the approach which would find most favour with those groups who had been pressing for change. However it would be strongly criticised by those opposed to change who would see it as 'marking society's approval of homosexuality as an acceptable or parallel lifestyle'. Regarding the age of consent, the memo stated that 17 years would be the same as that for heterosexuals and was favoured by the homosexual community. Reference was made to other European countries with an equal age of consent.

> A common age of consent could however cause genuine problems for many people who are concerned about the alternative lifestyle promoted by the homosexual community. It could also provide encouragement for a campaign for recognition of what have been called 'the more bizarre manifestations of homosexuality' such as homosexual marriage.

The memo seemed to come down in favour of 18 years, the present age of majority and referred strangely to boys in boarding schools. In our contacts with officials over the years it seemed that they considered 18 as an attractive compromise as it would 'mark a difference' between heterosexuality and homosexuality. An age of consent of 21 was given short shrift.

It is not known who leaked the document or what their motives were, but according to Geraldine Kennedy of *The Irish Times*, who broke the story, the publication of the memo made the task of the Government in introducing reform far more troublesome. She continued that Mrs Geogeghan-Quinn must bear some of the responsibility for this development since the memo as a whole was 'a far cry from the spirit of the commitment to equality in the Programme for Government. The whole thrust of the memo is towards the most minimal change.' One of the more surprising aspects of the memo was that the LRC recommendations were regarded merely as an option at the radical end of the spectrum. The fact that this was the Government's own advisory body that had carried out extensive research and consultation and come forward with concensus-based recommendations did not seem to matter that much. As Fintan O'Toole put it in *The Irish Times*: 'It is astonishing . . . to find in the memo on homosexuality Mrs Geogeghan-Quinn is still presenting the problem as one which is defined by the existence of opposing pressure groups. One side, though unnamed, is Family Solidarity. The other side is pretty much everyone else.' GLEN expressed dismay that the Government was still considering the British legislation as a possible model: 'This would retain the criminal status of gay men, undermine the Government's strong commitment to equality and reverse the evolving and progressive policy in this area.' Indeed, in our rush to condemn the memo we almost forgot to welcome the fact that the Government was intent on introducing a law reform.

Strong support was received for the equality option in an *Irish Times* editorial and from writers in other newspapers, such as Colm Toibín and Bruce Arnold in the *Irish Independent*. While it is often presumed that the media are overwhelmingly in our favour, our experience is sometimes quite different. We had been hoping that RTE's *Prime Time* would produce the first current affairs programme on the lesbian and gay community, looking at which law reform should be introduced and what its effects would be on our society. Instead, we were put into a studio with those who might be described as the 'demented tendency' of the right-wing—Youth Defence. As Colm Toibín described it in the *Sunday Independent*: '. . . people who are demanding a fundamental civil right were being baited by people with contrary views. There was no chance of a rational debate. It was another small disaster in RTE's coverage of current affairs'.

The leak of the memo had a positive effect in that it sharpened the focus of the debate and energised our lobbying effort now that the choices had been put so starkly. By then we were involved in a hectic round of lobbying at the highest levels. We were excited by the drama but kept our eyes on the prize, never compromising on issues of equality (even behind closed doors). Our priority now was to insist on repeal of the common law offence and the 1861 and 1885 legislation. Indeed, we took a carefully calculated decision and made it known that we would call for the defeat of any Bill that did not involve the repeal of the 1861 and 1885 legislation and the common law offence. An equal age of consent of 17 years was also essential if we were not to make criminals of our young people. Legislation regarding sexual behaviour in public and other matters should make no distinction between homosexuality and hetero-sexuality as recommended by the LRC in other reports.

The equality commitment of the Government was a major argument, especially when Máire Geoghegan-Quinn, the Minister for Equality and other ministers were convinced of the linkage. Equality is a clear-cut principle: you either legislate for it or you legislate for inequality. The recommendations of the LRC, which provided for equality and the example of other European countries, who had equal laws, were also important arguments. Personal contacts, primarily with members of the Labour party, now came into play and the Labour members of the Cabinet made a joint response to the draft memo arguing for equality (*Sunday Tribune* 2.5.93). Stonewall (the English gay lobby group), Jeff Dudgeon and the Committee on the Administration of Justice from Northern Ireland all publicly advised against a British-style law reform. In a letter to the Minister for Justice, Jeff Dudgeon stated that the British law reform is 'discriminatory, unfair and antiquated'.

In early May, the Taoiseach made a firm declaration to reform the 'Victorian laws' on homosexuality. He refused however to commit himself on the age of consent or on the question of homosexuals in the defence forces. He added that there are many different lifestyles in our society and that within broad legal limits we have to trust our citizens to exercise freedom with responsibility'. Our intensive lobbying was having its effect and by mid-May, the *Irish Independent* was reporting that there was increasing support at Cabinet level for the more radical option. According to reports, the feeling was that those opposing change would do so anyway, regardless of the scope of the measures, and since the Government had committed itself to a major law reform and equality agenda, it had to take a firm stand on decriminalising homosexuality. The issue was now regarded as the first major test of the Government's nerve in the thorny area of legislation on social and moral issues. It had been thought that 18 might emerge as a possible compromise, but the Minister had decided, according to the newspaper report, that there should be equality with the age of consent for heterosexuals. While there were newspaper reports that 'the legislation seems certain to provoke a backlash from conservative deputies and outside groups opposed to change' (*II*, 19.5.93), an opinion poll in Dublin indicated that two thirds supported an equal age of consent, and on RTE radio Mrs Geoghegan-Quinn argued strongly for a law reform based on equality.

There was a last-minute alarm as a *Sunday Press* opinion poll found that 50 per cent were opposed to law reform with some 34 per cent in favour. However when the tide is running in your favour it seems that set-backs rebound to your advantage. The coverage in the *Irish Press* the next day was entirely positive and headlined 'Poll won't halt gay Bill before Dáil, say activists'. We had been warned a number of times over the years by people who had experience of dealing with the right-wing that 'You won't know what hit you when the Bill is published, they will crawl out from the woodwork.' Family Solidarity certainly unleashed more of their invective, stating that 'The proposal to legalise buggery for 17-year olds is repulsive and grossly irresponsible and parents will not buy it'. Furthermore, 'To legalise buggery and acts of gross indecency with teenagers . . . would be a corrupt and shameful piece of political toadyism in which the moral, emotional and physical health of the young would be seriously jeopardised in order to curry favour with the gays themselves.'

We were always surprised that Family Solidarity never argued for a restrictive reform and instead continued to oppose any law reform even when this was clearly a lost cause. Right up until the end, they were recommending that no law reform was necessary and that Ireland should seek a derogation from the ECHR. As it turned out the expected backlash did not materialise. According to one political correspondent, the last minute campaign by Family Solidarity to rally support for a rejection of the legislation 'failed spectacularly'. The Catholic Church had strongly opposed progress for lesbians and gay men but a few days before the Bill was published issued a moderate statement that it 'does not expect that acts which are sinful should, by that very fact, be made criminal offenses'. While many lesbians and gay men would take exception to their relationships being described as sinful, GLEN welcomed the conciliatory tone of the statement and in fact in a letter to all the bishops, it had encouraged the Church to make such a distinction between Church teaching and State law. In our letter we had also pointed out that we would be on the same side on other matters of social and economic justice. We were to receive a number of replies from bishops thanking us for our 'helpful' and 'constructive' briefing documents and for our 'appreciation of the many things we have in common'. As one senator put it, 'The strident lashing of the flock seems to be a thing of the past.' On 23 June the Minister for Justice proposed the Criminal Law (Sexual Offences) Bill 1993 to the Dáil which provided for equality between heterosexuals and homosexuals. In a powerful speech she stated that: 'In other areas of public concern and debate in this country we have come to appreciate the need to recognise, respect and value difference.' In the same month the Oireachtas passed Bills decriminalising suicide and providing for the extensive availability of condoms. Unfortunately the gay law reform bill included provisions to recriminalise prostitution including the clients.

In what may at the time have seemed like a good tactic to embarrass the Coalition, Fine Gael decided to put down an amendment to raise the age of consent to 18 years. This horrified many of their deputies, especially those whom we had worked with on equality issues. Deputies Alan Shatter, Nora Owen (Deputy Leader of the Party) and Mary Flaherty were carrying out what seemed like an organised filibuster. With just fifteen minutes remaining before the Bill passed all stages in the Dáil on Thursday 24th June, the amendment to raise the age of consent had not been reached. The Progressive Democrats offered to withdraw their amendement so that the FG amendment could be put and FG embarrassed. Alan Shatter called for a vote on the PD amendment and as this used up the twelve minutes remaining for debate on amendments, the FG amendment automatically fell without being moved. The Independent TD Johnny Fox was the only deputy to call for a vote when the final stages of the Bill were put to the House. Since no one supported him, the Bill passed all stages without a vote. Signs in the Visitors Gallery prohibit any laughing, applause or even reading but when the Ceann Comhairle announced that the Bill had passed, Phil Moore of Parents Enquiry led a brief cheer and applause. Ruairí Quinn, a senior Government Minister looked up and gave us the clenched fist salute.

As a society we had faced up to our fear of sexuality, especially a different sexuality, and made a radical choice on the basis of an optimistic view of human nature. The law reform was about a respect for heterosexuality as much for homosexuality. For many heterosexuals, the bleak and narrow vision of Family Solidarity was seen as personally threatening. The reforms are an important step in healing the shame we experience in general as Irish people and, in particular, in terms of sexuality. As Nora Owen said in the Dáil, 'I do not believe that there is anything as fundamental, apart from the right to life, as the right to our sexuality, which is our very essence and makes us what we are.'

For many lesbians and gay men, the law reform has had a powerful liberating effect on our sense of ourselves. It is like a great burden being lifted from our shoulders, a burden we had grown up with and had hardly realised existed. Coincidentally the annual Lesbian and Gay Pride Parade was held on the following Saturday. In her column in *The Irish Times* Mary Holland wrote:

> One would need a heart of stone not to have been moved by the great waves of happiness that surged through the centre of Dublin last Saturday afternoon as Irish lesbians and gays took to the streets. They threw pink carnations into the crowd, walked hand in hand and chanted 'We're here, we're queer, we're legal'.

I had the great honour to address the ecstatic crowds outside the Central Bank at the end of the parade; I reminded them that:

> We all had a dream that one balmy summers day we would celebrate being full and equal citizens of this Irish Republic. This is the day. It is a victory for all those struggling for equality in this country. These reforms are a great achievement for Irish society and for its lesbian and gay community; so we can stand here today proud to be Irish and proud to be lesbian and gay.

5. THE FUTURE

> The original idea of feminism as I first encountered it, in about 1969, was . . . that nothing short of equality will do and that in society marred by injustice and cruelty, equality will never be good enough. (Barbara Ehreneich, 1991.)

SOCIAL AND ECONOMIC PARTNERSHIP

While the equality-based law reform is fundamentally important in removing the taint of criminality, it must be remembered that it only provides the basis for achieving equality in people's everyday lives. This has been accepted by the Government and an amended Employment Equality Act and a new Equal Status Bill are to be introduced in the near future.

Under the proposed equal status legislation, it will be unlawful to discriminate in education, in the provision of goods, facilities and services and in the disposal of accommodation or other premises. The legislation will specifically include all the vulnerable groups and it is suggested that handicap or disability could be defined so as to include being HIV positive. Direct and indirect discrimination would also be included. It is proposed that the Equality Commission will replace the Employment Equality Agency and its membership extended to reflect its expanded responsibilities.

This legislation will significantly improve the quality of life for a substantial proportion, if not the majority, of Irish people, if one includes all women together with gay men, Travellers, people with disabilities and other categories of people who are vulnerable to discrimination. It is a significant achievement for all the campaigning groups who over many years built a consensus that such inclusive legislation was necessary and politically feasible. In particular, it is an achievement for those lesbians and gay men who have always argued and campaigned for anti-discrimination legislation, not just for lesbians and gay men but for every group subject to discrimination. It is also a great step forward for Irish society in giving practical effect to the egalitarian principles expressed in the 1916 Proclamation of the Republic and the Constitution and in the republican ideals of equal citizenship. This renewed commitment to equality should bolster our civic culture which is, according to some commentators, endangered by the declining in fluence of religion and nationalism.

The legislation will transform the possibilities for the lesbian and gay community in Ireland, not least because it will empower people to believe that they are entitled to be treated fairly, without prejudice or discrimination. In that sense, one of the most important effects of the legislation will be to develop a climate of equality that will tend to make discrimination socially unacceptable. In Spain, a mass education campaign was carried out using slogans such as 'Democracia es Iqualdad' and 'Igualdad para vivir, diver sidad para convivir'.

However, experience with both gender equality legislation in the twenty-six counties and with religious anti-discrimination legislation in the six counties shows that there is an infrastructure of discrimination which is extremely difficult to dismantle and which can reproduce itself in different guises. The success of the new legislation will depend on its exact terms as well as the powers and resources given to the Commission and its determination to effectively challenge powerful vested interests when necessary. The willingness of state agencies to implement equality programmes will also be crucial. Given the strangle-hold that the Catholic Church has over education, health and some community/youth services in Ireland, a wide religious exemption would fatally undermine the legislation (GLEN, 1993c).

Two issues that are often seen as particularly controversial are the recognition of lesbian and gay domestic partnerships and matters relating to custody, parenting and adoption of children. As regards the latter, it is clear that the rights of the child should be the primary consideration and that the sexual orientation of the adult should not be a consideration in assessing their ability to care for the child. The issue of the legal recognition of domestic partnership is less clear. A significant form of discrimination against lesbians and gay men in relation to pensions, public housing, taxation, immigration and other matters arises from the fact that our relationships are not legally recognised. While many lesbians and gay men are in long-standing couple relationships, it is also true that most lesbians and gay men rely more on friendship and community support networks than on lifetime coupledom. Whether and how partnerships should be recognised is the subject of much debate within the lesbian and gay community. Denmark and Norway have provided for the separate legal recognition of domestic partnerships for lesbians and gay men only (which excludes adoption) but this format is strongly criticised because it mimics a type of heterosexual relationship which many see as being based on economic dependency and control and one which many heterosexuals are rejecting. It seems that our political efforts should be devoted to building a society which will allow the lesbian and gay community to flourish. This is a political project antithetical to the Right, as Margaret Thatcher put it: 'There is no such thing as society, there are individuals and there are families.'

In a classic essay 'Capitalism and the Family', John D'Emilio (1992) has argued that while the economics of capitalism are undermining the role of the family, the ideology of capitalist society 'has enshrined the family as the source of love, affection, and emotional security, the place where our need for stable intimate human relationships is satisfied'. Lesbians, gay men and heterosexual feminists have become the scapegoats for the current instability of 'the family' and for that sense of impermanence and insecurity that people are now experiencing in their relationships. He suggests that 'we need political solutions for these difficulties of personal life'. We need structures and programmes that will help to dissolve the boundaries that isolate the family, particularly those that privatise childcare. We need to create structures beyond the nuclear family, structures to provide a sense of belonging and reinforce our emotional security.

In this respect, according to D'Emilio, gay people have a special role to play. Already excluded from families as most of us are, we have had to create for our survival 'networks of support that do not depend on the bonds of blood or the licence of the state, but that are freely chosen and nurtured'. The building of an 'affectional community' must be as much part of our political movement as are campaigns for civil rights. In this way we may prefigure the shape of personal relationships in a society grounded in equality and justice rather than exploitation and oppression, 'a society where autonomy and security do not preclude each other but coexist'.

The Second Commission on the Status of Women and the Kilkenny Incest Report recommended constitutional amendments to ensure the equal rights of women and children respectively and clearly all other disadvantaged groups should be given specific constitutional protection. In general, it can be said that any progress towards greater equality in Irish society and greater democratic rights or civil liberties for Irish citizens will directly benefit gay people. Any progress for particular disadvantaged groups such as Travellers or people with disabilities will directly benefit those lesbians and gay men who are in those categories and will indirectly benefit all gay people by enhancing a culture of equality and respect for difference.

While anti-discrimination legislation is vital, it is not sufficient in itself because it cannot dismantle the causes of discrimination let alone undermine the structures of a capitalist society which produces poverty and inequality. It is estimated that about 30 per cent of the Irish population lives in poverty. According to the Combat Poverty Agency (1993), 'Poverty and social exclusion are growing phenomena not only in Ireland but across the European Community. The extraordinarily rapid pace of economic, technological and social change over the past decade . . . (has) . . . widened the gap between the better off and those living in poverty'. What is also necessary is a broad economic and social programme to deal with the causes of inequality and disadvantage. Unemployment, low-wage and other marginalised employment is a primary cause of disadvantage and poverty. For the sake of emphasis, one could say that a full-employment, high-wage economy would do more for the lesbian and gay community, not just in terms of economic independence, but also in that sense of freedom and assertiveness that it entails. Also, expanding the legal rights of workers, such as minimum wage legislation, and a strong and responsive trade-union movement are directly in the interests of lesbians and gay men.

These broad economic and social programmes must be informed by an understanding of the dynamics of disadvantage as it affects particular groups. This is the rationale for a recent research project entitled *Poverty and Lesbians and Gay Men* (GLEN 1993a). This study, funded by the Combat Poverty Agency, investigates those processes of discrimination which are likely to increase the risk of, or reinforce, poverty amongst lesbians and gay men and examines the various strategies which lesbians and gay men use to counter this discrimination. The study looks at five main areas of discrimination: unemployment and employment, education and youth services, housing and homelessness, social infrastructure, and harassment and violence. The study recognises that for a significant number of individuals, including many women, especially lesbian mothers, people with disabilities, the young and the elderly, Travellers and others, life-choices are extremely restricted; they have to conceal their sexuality or else face severe disadvantages.

One of the themes of the evolution of lesbian and gay politics in Ireland is the articulation of general principles and analyses to include a lesbian and gay perspective and the poverty study is the most recent example. There was a definite initial surprise, even resistance, amongst many people (including gay people) at the linking of the issues of poverty and discrimination against lesbians and gay men. A developing stereotype of gay people is that we are a homogenous minority: affluent, organised and male. There is in other countries a recurring media interest in the 'the pink pound' and the 'pink economy', promoted no doubt by businesses that cater to gay people. There is clearly a niche for gay people in the capitalist system as consumers and this can be of the greatest importance in terms of the goods and services that can be bought, such as books, magazines, videos and services such as 'gay bars'. It has to be said that Irish capitalists have been true to form and are remarkably reluctant to be enterprising in terms of the lesbian/gay community. However, even when the market economy does respond, it is based on the consumers' ability to pay and not on their needs and it is likely that many lesbians and gay men would be excluded especially in Ireland where poverty and unemployment are so widespread.

This poverty research is pioneering in international terms and is the most recent example of how the Irish lesbian and gay movement has developed its own particular analysis and strategies appropriate to Irish circumstances. Ironically, the 'rediscovery' of poverty in Ireland could be said to stem at least in part from the work of the social justice wing of the Catholic Church, in particular a conference on poverty organised by the Church in 1971. It also reflects the determined efforts of the Combat Poverty Agency in putting the issue of poverty on the political agenda and the recent feminist analyses which highlighted the links between discrimination and poverty amongst women. Equally important are the socialist commitments of those centrally involved in the Irish lesbian and gay movement and the research report will provide the basis for a socialist lesbian and gay economic analysis.

It is widely accepted now that a strategy to combat disadvantage must include significant support for community development at a local level. For the past twenty years various lesbian and gay community services have continued to provide basic support for thousands of people with little or no outside funding or other assistance. In fact, many of these services have faced considerable opposition in terms of obtaining funding, premises and in advertising their services. One consequence of this lack of respectability is that it has allowed our community to develop its own initiatives, free from outside manipulation and control, an autonomy denied to other disadvantaged communities.

It is clear that there is now an urgent need for an equal partnership between the lesbian and gay community and the various state and other agencies in order to respond to the many needs and opportunities which currently exist. For this partnership to be genuine and productive the lesbian and gay community sector must be resourced by the State so that it can effectively carry out its work and participate on an equal basis with outside agencies. This in turn requires that the lesbian and gay community evolve democratic and accountable structures and agreed policies at a national level. This is a complex and difficult task given the diversity of needs and perspectives within our communities but it cannot be avoided if we are to move confidently into that space created by the work of the past twenty years. As in 1988, when the equality programme of GLEN was agreed, we could now develop an optimistic but feasible programme of community action which would radically improve the lives of lesbians and gay men. We cannot use the excuse that dramatic progress is not possible in this country; what we now face are the responsibilities and problems of success. One of these problems is how to work within the system without abandoning a long-term vision of social transformation.

The recommendations of the Poverty Study will provide the basis for preparing a community development programme and will no doubt involve a wide range of initiatives including community centres, workers cooperatives, community enterprises and other job-creation projects, housing cooperatives, education and training schemes, health projects and a variety of social support services. The development of proper community facilities will be extremely important in the fight against the spread of HIV and AIDS. In Australia the Government endorsed the AIDS Council's approach, which saw its role as fostering individual self-esteem and gay community development. The idea was that the better individual gay men felt about themselves and the stronger their community support systems were, the more likely they would be to practice safer sex and to lead healthy lives. It seems that the Department of Health here now supports such an analysis and will fund action-research projects on the role of the gay community and its needs.

An essential element of such community development is a cultural programme. 'The economic system has not only excluded citizens from necessities like adequate housing,' according to Michael D. Higgins, 'it has also excluded them from their own stories about themselves, from their own dreams and imaginations.' In a speech in Derry, the Minister for Arts, Culture and the Gaeltacht developed this theme further and said that 'Every person should be able to tell their own story and the rest of us should be patient and tolerant enough to listen'. There is already a burgeoning lesbian and gay culture, with its own film festival in Cork and writers such as Mary Dorcey, Emma Donoghue and Desmond Hogan and musicians such as Zrazy as well as community theatre and festivals. These cultural projects can be justified in their own terms but they also have practical effects; as Edmund White put it, if we tell the stories of our lives we are 'not just reporting the past but also shaping the future, forging an identity as much as revealing it'.

One issue which cannot and should not be avoided is the intractable, problematic and delightful issue of sex, an issue which, as D'Emilio put it, 'taps into the deepest layers of human and social irrationality' and which makes the gay community vulnerable to attack. The media frenzy during the recent 'Phoenix Park controversy' involving a junior Minister, a young man and the Guards is a prime example. The overall outcome of the controversy was positive in that there was considerable public support for the Minister, the media coverage was generally fair and there was no scapegoating of the gay community. The lesbian and gay movement is different from other emancipatory movements in that issues of sexuality are central and unavoidable. In a great introduction to *The Faber Book of Gay Short Fiction*, Edmund White writes that if one of the main impulses behind gay fiction is avowal and self discovery, another is surely sexual affirmation. He describes how in James Baldwin's story 'Just Above My Head,' the young men look at each other 'with a real hunger, a simple wonder before the flesh of another man, so similar and yet so radically different: a miracle of spinal column, neck to buttocks, shoulders and shoulder blades, elbows, wrists, thighs, ankles, a miracle of bone and blood and muscle and flesh and music'. This simple catechism, he states, is one the gay lover never tires of telling, 'a language that has been suppressed as often as it was invented and that must be created again and again'.

THE NEED FOR INTERNATIONAL ACTION

Amnesty International in recent reports states that:

> Protecting the human rights of gays and lesbians is an international responsibility . . . and is a struggle to be waged by all people, just as the struggle for human rights for women, for indigenous peoples, for refugees, for the disappeared, and for the survivors of torture is an international responsibility and is waged by all people. . . . Homosexuals in many parts of the world live in constant fear of government persecution–afraid that their private acts of love and public acts of courage will be punished by governments in secret torture chambers, at clandestine 'safe houses', and on midnight raids.

There is increasing documentation of persecution of homosexuals. The methods used include unfair trials and imprisonment, cruel and degrading practices, torture (including rape) to the ultimate sanction of judicial and extrajudicial executions. In Colombia, for example, killings of so-called 'social undesirables' such as street-children and homosexuals continue to be reported. Victims of these 'death squads' are gunned down in the streets at night or seized and driven away in unmarked cars. Their bodies, which are rarely identified, often bear signs of torture. The perpetrators of these acts have frequently been identified as members of the National Police. When lesbians and gay men are targeted in such operations, they are at high risk, with little or no social or political support available to expose, denounce or stop the abuses. The consequences of speaking out may be as bad or worse than keeping quiet: in one case, a bisexual man in Brazil was tortured and killed after seeking official protection from his would-be assassins. The Iranian authorities have reiterated publicly that the death penalty is a possible punishment for persons found guilty of homosexual acts. In Romania, gay men have been routinely targeted for ill-treatment and torture. Amnesty International have also received reports of the ill-treatment of gay people in the US and Turkey.

For many years, lesbians and gay men campaigned alone, through the International Lesbian and Gay Association (ILGA), on behalf of those persecuted. However in 1991 after years of debate, Amnesty extended its mandate to include as prisoners of conscience gay people imprisoned because of their consenting sexual relationships. The Irish section had at its previous AGM overwhelmingly adopted a similar policy and the Irish delegates played a significant lobbying role at the international conference in Yokohama. It seems that Ireland's status as a post-colonial and Catholic country makes our support for the rights of lesbians and gay men more acceptable to countries who would be resistant to what might be seen as the cultural insensitivities of the US or northern Europe. It would be difficult to overestimate the importance of the work now being carried out by Amnesty International; it is a lifeline for many lesbians and gay men throughout the world, a reminder that they are not forgotten. Another policy development which should prove equally important is the decision of the UN Committee on Human Rights in 1994 that the Tasmanian anti-gay legislation contravenes the UN Declaration of Human Rights.

The western colonising countries were often shocked by the acceptance of homosexuality that they found amongst those whom they colonised and Britain especially exported its homophobic laws to those countries. Ironically many of these countries now regard homosexuality as a foreign implant. According to one South African lesbian 'People say "Its white people who are gay. You're not gay. You're African. Its not part of your culture"'[11] More recent economic and sometimes military imperialism particularly against Islamic countries fuels a fundamentalist reaction which is inimical to women and gay people. In other cases, national liberation movements have been strongly influenced by a form of Stalinism, which is also hostile to gay people with Castro's Cuba being a notorious example. However, under pressure from gay activists within their ranks, the ANC and to a lesser extent Nicaragua's FSLN are supportive of the rights of lesbians and gay men. After many years of determined destabilisation by the Reagan administration and other right-wing elements, what little progress had been made in Nicaragua under the Sandinistas was lost when the new US inspired regime introduced a draconian anti-gay law in 1992. Article 205 of the Penal Code now provides that 'anyone who induces, promotes, propagandises or practises in scandalous form sexual intercourse between persons of the same sex commits the crime of sodomy and shall incur 1 to 3 years imprisonment'.

The Irish government has been supportive of initiatives for the rights of gay people at an international level, such as the recognition of ILGA at the UN in 1993. However it could do a great deal more valuable work at the UN and within other international organisations such as the European Union, the Council of Europe, the International Labour Organisation, Conference on Security and Co-operation in Europe. It is evident that the Irish law reform will have an effect in Europe, as Jeff Dudgeon, who took the Northern Ireland case to the European Court of Human Rights, wrote shortly afterwards:

'it will be both a spur and a magnet in Whitehall if the
recognition grows that the UK has been upstaged by a
new Ireland that is no longer given a fool's pardon for
Catholic excess, but can instead swank around Brussels
with a modern image.'

(The ongoing harassment of gay men in the North is an issue
which should be taken up now by the Minister for Justice under the
Anglo-Irish Agreement.) In its proposed asylum legislation, the
Government could specifically include those who are persecuted
because of their sexual orientation by clarifying that the term 'social
group' referred to in the Convention on Refugees includes a group
based on sexual orientation. In addition, through its Third World
development programmes, it could practically assist the emerging
lesbian and gay community groups in many parts of the Third
World, especially Latin America, and in the former soviet block
countries. There is also a significant role here for the various Irish
Third World organisations in supporting the many human rights
and community development initiatives in these countries. For
some people this proposal may extend their understanding of the
issues too far. I remember suggesting at an Irish Nicaragua Support
Group conference that the various Irish social movements, such as
the gay movement, could be mobilised to support their comrades
in Nicaragua. For one left-wing stalwart this was incomprehen-
sible, turning around, she asked me in a bemused tone 'What has
gay rights got to do with Nicaragua?'

While the lesbian and gay movements in the advanced capitalist
countries have led the way in creating the possibility of a lesbian and
gay identity and politics, there is the possibility that their dominance
may hinder the emergence of an indigenous lesbian and gay culture
and politics in other countries. Ireland may have a particular
bridging role to play because it is a post-colonial and economically
peripheral country which has close links with the lesbian and gay

71

movements in Britain and the US. For a small country we have already made a significant contribution to the international lesbian and gay community, not least through our many emigrants who have become activists in their new countries. We could develop particular links with other small, peripheral, post-colonial societies such as Tasmania which has been experiencing a contentious law reform campaign since 1988. According to Rodney Croome, a leader of that campaign, if Australia as a whole had an inferiority complex, in Tasmania the insecurities were magnified tenfold. Tasmania was a national joke for mainland Australians who projected all their own fears, insecurities and self-doubts onto the island. However, in the 1970s and the early 1980s, the island underwent a transformation. It became the focus of environmental conflict in a very environmentally conscious country. The sense of empowerment that so many Tasmanians felt as a result of the Franklin Dam campaign extended to gays and lesbians as well. 'If it weren't for the Green movement', said Rodney Croome, 'I don't think there would have been any gay politics in Tasmania. Tasmanian society is so homogenous. But the Green subculture . . . provided a refuge to some extent for people who did not fit into the mainstream. And the Green movement also provided us with expertise and resources'. He concludes that:

> 'Until 1988, gay life in Tasmania was as hidden and
> invisible and as limiting as you could find in this
> country. Today we are working on creating a gay
> Tasmanian identity. In the past to have a gay identity
> you had to leave the island. If you stayed you lived in
> fear and hiding. We are trying to make it possible to
> live in Tasmania as a gay person. We are achieving this
> to a remarkable extent.' (Miller, 1992)

CONCLUSION

Solidarity is a two-way process and we have as much to learn and to gain as to give. We have already gained considerably through our involvement with ILGA not least in that sense of hope from taking part in an organisation made up of ordinary people from all over the world which is a miracle of effective international cooperation, based on trust and generosity and little or no money or bureaucracy. Taking part in the First Irish Coffee Brigade to Nicaragua in 1988, I was privileged to hear Tomas Borge, the only surviving founder-member of the FSLN who himself had been tortured and whose wife had died under torture, address the World Conference of Indigenous Peoples on international solidarity, which he described as 'the tenderness of the peoples'.

The granting of equal citizenship to lesbians and gay men expands the confidence of Irish society to deal with other controversial issues on a rational and principled basis. It is a welcome sign that we will not only tolerate but welcome diversity and equality in our society. This new found equality has liberated the energy of the lesbian and gay community and there is now the opportunity for a much more creative relationship with the wider community. As a society we have come a long way, and while many issues have yet to be resolved, it seems that we can look to the future with great hope.

NOTES

1. Much of the material in this chapter is based on personal experience and also to a great extent on *Out for Ourselves* by the Dublin Lesbian and Gay Mens Collectives. Other sources are the ICCL, Joni Crone, Eileen Evason and 'The Importance of being Lesbian' by Eilis Mhara in *Political Records, Thirty Years of Lesbian and Gay History*, B. Cant and S. Hemmings (eds).

2. See Maguire (1993); W.J.Walsh, 'Everyone should be allowed to march tomorrow', *The Irish Times* 16.3.92; Liam Fay, 'Exiles on Main Street', *Hot Press*, 26.2.1992; Helena Mulkerns, 'Marchers 17-Hibernians 0', *Hot Press*, 12.3.1993; 'Save the Parade', *Irish Voice*, Vol. 6 No.8, 25 February 1992; Marie Crowe, 'Being Irish and Gay: the US experience', *The Sunday Tribune*, 17 March 1991; Mary Holland, 'Parading gays and lesbians make the law look an absolute ass', *The Irish Times*, 26 March 1992; Nuala O'Faolain, 'New York could learn a lesson from St Patricks Day in Cork', *The Irish Times*, 15 March 1993 and extensive other media coverage.

3. The 1861 Act was in fact a reform of previous seventeenth-century legislation which provided for the death penalty. The criminalisation of sexual relationships between men was introduced into Ireland as part of the process of colonisation with the introduction of common law and also by 'An Act for the Punishment of the Vice of Buggery' passed by the Irish House of Commons in 1634. This law was merely transferring to Ireland an English statute of 1533 which made sodomy a felony for men, which the criminal courts could punish by death; previously, sodomy trials were held in ecclesiastical courts. Section 61 of the 1861 Act comes under the heading of 'Unnatural Offences' as amended by the Statute Law Reform Act 1892, S. 61 provides: 'Whoever shall be convicted of the abominable crime of buggery, committed with mankind or with animal, shall be liable to be kept in penal servitude for life.' Under S. 62 of the 1861 Act, 'whoever shall attempt to commit the said abominable crime, or shall be guilty of any assault with intent to commit the same, or of any indecent assault upon the any male person, shall be guilty of a mis-demeanour, and being convicted thereof, shall be kept in penal servitude for any term, not exceeding ten years.' Section 11 of the Act of 1885 is included in Part 1 of the Act under the heading 'Protection of Women and Girls'. It reads: 'Any person who, in public or private, comits, or is party to the commission of, or procures or attempts to procure the commission by any male person of, any act of gross indecency with another male person, shall be guilty of a misdemeanour, and be convicted thereof, shall be liable at

the discretion of the court to be imprisoned for any term not exceeding two years, with or without hard labour.'

4. See ICCL op.cit; Conor Gearty, 'Constitutional Law–Homosexuals and the Criminal Law: The Right to Privacy', *Dublin University Law Journal* (DULJ) 1983, pp. 264-273; and A.M. Connelly, 'Irish Law and the Judgement of the European Court of Human Rights in the Dudgeon Case' *DULJ*, 1982, pp. 25-40.

5. Joe Carroll, 'O'Higgins favours extradition change', *The Irish Times*, 8.10.1991, p. 10; Gearty, op.cit.

6. See Stephen Jeffrey-Poulter, *Peers, Queers and Commons, The Struggle for Gay Law Reform from 1950 to the Present*, Routledge, 1991, pp. 147–154; Jeff Dudgeon, 'The U.K. Supreme Court', *The Socialist*, Summer 1984, pp. 14-15.

7. The debate took a strange turn when Pat McCartan proposed that the definition of rape should also include penetration of the anus by an object. Rape was defined so as to include penetration of the anus or mouth by the penis. Vaginal rape included penetration of the vagina by any object. The proposal seems reasonable but the Minister disagreed, stating that 'The answer is simple. Penetration of an anus by an object does not involve a sexual organ. Such penetration is not intrinsically sexual. Indeed depending on the circumstances it might not even constitute an indecent assault under existing law.'

8. In fact there seems to be some evidence that the Protocol which resulted in all the trouble may have been caused, at least in part, by right-wing concerns that the EC Commission was proposing that the EC accede to the European Convention on Human Rights. Such a step could mean that decisions of the Court of Human Rights could be 'forced into Irish domestic law by the EC, which can automatically override the Irish constitution' according to the newsletter of one right-wing group The Responsible Society. At the time, these concerns as raised in the FF-PD coalition, it 'was taken at the time to be a reference to the judgement in the Norris case, which would oblige the Irish laws against homosexual acts to be changed, but it is now clear that abortion was also seen as relevant.' (*IT*, 17.6.92)

SUGGESTIONS FOR FURTHER READING

While there has been an explosion of material being published on lesbian and gay issues internationally, very little has been published relating to Ireland, at least until recently. *Out for Ourselves* produced by the Dublin lesbian and Gay mens Collectives was a major achievement when it was published in 1986 but is now sadly out of print. The Irish Council for Civil Liberties 'Equality Now for Lesbians and Gay Men' is a well-researched campaigning document with trenchant criticisms of the High and Supreme Courts' decisions at its heart. *Poverty and Lesbians and Gay Men* is a major forthcoming study carried out by GLEN, with Combat Poverty Agency funding, into the links between discrimination and poverty. The Dáil and Senate debates are wide ranging, fascinating and funny. The forthcoming fourth volume of the *Field Day Anthology of Irish Writing* will include lesbian and gay material. *Ordinary People Dancing*, edited by Eibhear Walshe, is a good example of Irish lesbian and gay scholarship. *Gay Community News* is a free monthly, published by the National Lesbian and Gay Federation, and contains a full listing of all lesbian and gay services. *Quare Times*, *Out* and *Identity* are now defunct magazines and these, along with other invaluable archive material, are stored in the archive of the Hirschfield Centre. *The Abortion Papers* (Smyth), *Understanding Contemporary Ireland* (Breen et al.), *Masterminds of the Right* (O'Reilly), *Feminism in Ireland* (Smyth) and of course Joe Lee's magnum opus all provide an essential background for understanding developments in terms of lesbian/gay issues.

It is very difficult to keep up with the accelerating production of written material on lesbian and gay issues, but *Modern Homosexualities*, edited by Ken Plummer, is a good introduction to academic studies in a range of countries and contains a comprehensive bibliography. Of all the recently published works, the one I enjoyed the most is *Hometowns, 28 US Gay Men Writing Candidly About Where They Came From, Why They Left, and Where They Ended Up*. Anything by D'Emilio,

Watney, Weeks and Altman is worth reading and D'Emilio's collection *Making Trouble* is great, and not just because of its title. *Psychological Perspectives on Lesbian and Gay Male Experience*, edited by Garnets and Kimmel, is a comprehensive academic study relating to youth, ageing, relationships, health, violence, etc. Gay and lesbian life from Europe to Africa, Asia and Australia is the subject of 'Out in the World' a good journalistic account by Neil Miller. *Safety in Numbers* by Edmund King is a well-documented and essential guide to the gay mens' safer sex movement in Britain. *Sustaining Safe Sex: Gay Communities Respond to AIDS*, edited by Susan Kippax, is a good account of the Australian situation, which is a model for us here. *Homosexuality: A European Community Issue*, edited by Waaldjik and Clapham, is as exciting as its title but is an invaluable source book. A good overview of recent historical research is found in *Hidden from History*, edited by Dubermann and others, and includes articles on Asia, Africa, Latin-America. *Lesbian (Out)Law* by Ruthann Robson is a subversive perspective on legal issues. *Slow Motion* by Lynne Segal is a comprehensive analysis of masculinities, homophobia and racism and the prospects of change from a socialist/feminist perspective. There is an almost unstoppable flood of books, which ask questions like 'But what does it mean to say someone is gay? A dyke? A queen? Queer?'; *Inside/Out*, edited by Diana Fuss is one such anthology. *Perverts in Paradise*, by Joao Trevisan is one of the few accounts of gay life from a Third World (Brazilian) perspective that is available in English. *In the Life*, edited by Beam, and *Living the Spirit*, edited by Roscoe, are US black gay and gay American Indian anthologies respectively. The second ILGA Pink Book provides a much-needed global perspective. There is now a huge volume of gay and lesbian fiction and the companion *Penguin* Books *of Gay* and *Lesbian Short Stories* are accessible introductions (the former is edited by David Leavitt and Mark Mitchell and the latter by Margaret Reynolds).

BIBLIOGRAPHY

Amnesty International (1993) *First Steps: Amnesty International's Work On Behalf Of Lesbians And Gay Men*; London Amnesty International (1994), *Breaking the Silence: Human Rights Violations Based on Sexual Orientation*, New York

Bad Object-Choices (ed.), (1991), *How Do I Look? Queer Film and Video*, Seattle: Bay Press

Barry, Ursula, (1992) 'Movement, change and reaction: the struggle over reproductive rights in Ireland' in A. Smyth

Beam J. (1986) *In The Life: A Black Gay Anthology*, Boston: Alyson

Boswell J. (1980) *Christianity, Social Tolerance and Homosexuality, Gay People in Western Europe from the Beginning of the Christian Era to the Fourteenth Century*, Chicago: University of Chicago Press

Bray A. (1982) *Homosexuality in Renaissance England*, London: GMP

Breen R. et al., *Understanding Contemporary Ireland, State Class and Development in the Republic of Ireland*, Dublin: Gill and Macmillan

Cant B. and Hemmings S. eds. (1988) *Radical Records: Thirty Years of Lesbian and Gay History*, London: Routledge

Combat Poverty Agency (1992) *Annual Report*, Dublin: Combat Poverty

Connolly J. (1914) 'Labour and the Proposed Partition of Ireland', *Irish Worker*, 14 March 1914, republished in James Connolly, *Selected Writing*, ed. Peter Beresford Ellis, Harmondsworth: Penguin

Crone J. (1988) 'Lesbian Feminism in Ireland' in A. Smyth (1988)

Dail Eireann, Criminal Law (Sexual Offences) Bill 1993: Parliamentary Debates, Vol. 432, Nos. 7 and 8

D'Emilio J. (1983) *Sexual Politics, Sexual Communities, The Making of Homosexual Minority in the United States, 1940–1970*, Chicago: Chicago University Press

D'Emilio J. and Freedman E. B. *Intimate Matters, A History of Sexuality in America*, New York: Harper and Row

D'Emilio J. (1992) *Making Trouble, Essays on Gay History, Politics and the University*, London: Routledge

Duberman M.B. et al. (eds.) (1991) *Hidden From History, Reclaiming the Gay and Lesbian Past*, London: Penguin

Dublin Lesbian and Gay Mens Collectives (1986) *Out for Ourselves, The Lives of Irish Lesbians and Gay Men*, Dublin: Womens Community Press (out of print)

Dudgeon J. (1993) '*Ireland's Success; England's Opportunity?*', Belfast: mimeo.

Dudgeon J. (1984) 'The UK Supreme Court', *The Socialist*, Summer 1984

Ehrenreich B. (1991) *The Worst Years of Our Lives: Irreverent Notes From a Decade of Greed* Lime Tree (USA)

European Court of Human Rights, Judgement of the Court of 22 October 1981, Dudgeon, Series A, No. 45

European Court of Human Rights, Judgement of the Court of 26 October 1988, Norris, Series A, No. 142

Evason, Eileen (1991) *Against the Grain: The Contemporary Womens Movement in Northern Ireland*, Dublin: Attic Press,

Family Solidarity (1990) *The Homosexual Challenge: Analysis and Response*, Dublin: Family Solidarity

Farrell L.F. (ed.) (1993) *Lambda Gray: A Practical, Emotional, and Spiritual Guide for Gays and Lesbians who are Growing Older*, California: Newcastle Publishing

Foster R. (1989) *Modern Ireland 1600-1972*, London: Penguin

Foucault M. (1978) *The History of Sexuality: An Introduction*, London: Penguin

Fout J.C. and Tantillo M.S. (eds.) (1993) *American Sexual Politics: Sex, Gender and Race since the Civil War*, Chicago: The University of Chicago Press

Fuss D. (ed.) (1991) *Inside/Out: Lesbian Theories, Gay Theories*, London: Routledge

Gaffney G. (1991) *Glass Slippers and Tough Bargains: women, men and power*, Dublin: Attic Press

Garnets L., Kimmel D. (1973), *Psychological Perspectives on Lesbian and Gay Male Experiences*, New York: Columbia University Press

Gay and Lesbian Equality Network (1990) *Gay and Lesbian Equality*, Dublin: mimeo

Gay and Lesbian Equality Network (1992a) *Resource Material on Lesbian/Gay Law Reform*, Dublin: mimeo

Gay and Lesbian Equality Network (1992b), *Unfair Dismissals-Resource Material*, Dublin: mimeo

Gay and Lesbian Equality Network (1993a) *Poverty and Lesbians and Gay Men, A Research Proposal*, Dublin: mimeo

Gay and Lesbian Equality Network (1993b) *Asylum, Immigration and Sexual Orientation, Submission to Inter-departmental Committee on Non-Irish Nationals*, Dublin: mimeo

Gay and Lesbian Equality Network (1993c) *Equal Status Legislation, Submission to the Department of Equality and Law Reform*, Dublin: mimeo

Gay and Lesbian Equality Network (1994), *Proposed Action-Research Project on HIV Prevention Strategies and the Gay Community, A Submission to the Department of Health*, Dublin: mimeo

Gonsiorek C. and Weinrich J. (1990) *Homosexuality: Research Implications for Public Policy*, California: Sage

Gooding C. (1992) *Trouble With the Law? A Legal Handbook for Lesbians and Gay Men*, London: GMP

Herdt G. (ed.) (1989) *Gay and Lesbian Youth*, New York: Haworth Press

Herek G. and Berill K. (eds.) (1992) *Hate Crimes: Confronting Violence Against Lesbians and Gay Men*, London: Sage

Hodges A. and Hutten D. (1974) *With Downcast Gays: Aspects of Homosexual Oppression*, Toronto, Pink Triangle Press

Hyde H.M.(1972) *The Other Love: An Historical and Contemporary Survey of Homosexuality in Britain*, London: Mayflower

International Lesbian and Gay Association (1988) *The Second ILGA Pink Book: A Global View of Lesbian and Gay Liberation and Oppression*, Utrecht University

Irish Council for Civil Liberties (1990) *Equality Now for Lesbians and Gay Men*, Dublin: Irish Council for Civil Liberties

Jarman D., (1993) *At Your Own Risk: A Saint's Testament*, London: Vintage

Jeffrey-Poulter Stephen (1991) *Peers, Queers and Commons: The Struggle for Gay Law Reform from 1950 to the Present*, Routledge, London:

Kennedy G., 'Gay Law Change is Defined in Victorian Moral Terms', *The Irish Times*, 23 April, 1993

King E. (1993) *Safety in Numbers: Safer Sex and Gay Men*, London: Cassell

Kinsman G. (1987) *The Regulation of Desire: Sexuality in Canada*, Montreal: Black Rose

Kippax S. et al (1993) *Sustaining Safe Sex: Gay Communities Respond to AIDS*, London: Falmer Press

Kitzinger C. (1987) *The Social Construction of Lesbianism*, London: Sage

Kramer L. (1990) *Reports from the Holocaust: The Making of an AIDS Activist*, London: Penguin

Lauristen J. and Thorstad D. (1974) *The Early Homosexual Rights Movement (1864–1935)*, New York: Times Change Press

Law Reform Commission (1989) Consultation Paper On Child Sexual Abuse, Dublin

Law Reform Commission (1990) Report on Child Sexual Abuse, Dublin

Lee J.J. (1989) *Ireland 1912–1985, Politics and Society*, Cambridge: Cambridge University Press

Lynch B., (1993) *A Priest on Trial*, London: Bloomsbury

Maguire A. (1993) 'Friendly Sons of Saint Patrick?', *Irish Reporter* No. 10, second quarter

Marshall S. (1991) 'The Contemporary Political Use of Gay History: The Third Reich', in Bad Object-Choices (1991)

McCarroll J. 'The Case Against Homosexual Law Reform' *The Irish Times*, 23 April 1993

McCarroll J. 'Why Homosexual Acts Should Not be Legalised', *The Irish Times*, 30 May 1991

McClenaghan B. 'Invisible Comrades: Gays and Lesbians in the Struggle'. *The Captive Voice/An Glór Gafa*, Vol. 3 No. 3, Winter 1991

Miller N. (1993) *Out in the World, Gay and Lesbian Life from Buenos Aires to Bangkok*, England: Penguin

Names Project, The (1988) *The Quilt, Stories from the Names Project*, New York: Pocket Books

Norris D. (1981) 'Homosexual People and the Christian Churchs: A Minority and its Oppressors', *The Crane Bag*, Vol. 5 No. 1, Dublin

Norris v Attorney General (1984) I.R. 36

O'Reilly, E. (1992) *Masterminds of the Right*, Dublin: Attic Press

Parker A. et al. (eds.) (1992) *Nationalisms and Sexualities*, London: Routledge

Plummer K. (1992) *Modern Homosexualities: Fragments of Gay and Lesbian Experience*, London: Routledge

Ranke-Heineman U. (1988) *Eunuchs for Heaven: The Catholic Church and Sexuality*, London: Andre Deutsch

Robinson M. (1987) 'Women and the law in Ireland', in A. Smyth (ed.) (1988)

Robson C. 'Giving Equal Status to the Gay Community' *The Irish Times*, 26 March, 1993

Robson C. 'Homosexual Acts Should Not Be Crimes', *The Irish Times*, 19 July, 1991

Robson R. (1992) *Lesbian (Out)Law, Survival Under the Rule of Law*, Ithaca: Firebrand

Rose K. (1990) 'Lesbian and Gay' in *Alternative Ireland Directory*, Cork: Quay Co-op

Rose K. (1988) 'Lesbians and Gay Men' in *Nicaragua: An Unfinished Canvas*, Dublin: Nicaragua Book Collective

Rose K. (1989/90) 'In A Free State?' in *Rouge*, Issue No. 1, London: Rouge Publications

Rose K. (1991) 'The Fear of Diversity: Gay and Lesbian Rights' in *Irish Reporter*, Issue No. 2, second quarter 1991

Rose K. 'Defy Church Ruling on Homosexuals', *The Irish Times*, 17 August, 1992

Roscoe W. (1988) *Living the Spirit: A Gay American Indian Anthology*, New York: St Martins Press

Rowbotham S. (1973) *Hidden from History: 300 Years of Women's Oppression and the Fight Against it*, London: Pluto Press

Said E. W. (1993) *Culture and Imperialism*, London: Chatto and Windus

Seanad Éireann, European Court of Human Rights Judgement: Statements, Parliamentary Debates, Vol. 127 No. 1, 12 December 1990

Seanad Éireann, Criminal Law (Sexual Offences) Bill 1993 Parliamentary Debates, Vol. 137 Nos. 3 and 4

Second Commission on the Status of Women (1993), Report to Government, Stationery Office, Dublin

Segal L. (1990) *Slow Motion: Changing Masculinities, Changing Men*, London: Virago

Smyth A. (ed.) (1988) 'Feminism in Ireland', *Womens Studies International Forum*, Vol. 11 No. 4, New York

Smyth A. (ed.) (1992) *The Abortion Papers: Ireland*, Dublin: Attic Press

Smyth C. (1992) *Lesbians Talk Queer Notions*, London: Scarlet Press

Smyth, Marie, (1990) 'Kincora: Towards an Analysis', in *Gender, Sexuality and Social Control*, Bill Rolston and Mike Tomlinson (eds.), The European Group for the Study of Deviance and Social Control

Smyth, Marie (1991) 'Press Reporting of Kincora in Social Work', *The Media and Public Relations*, Bob Franklin and Nigel Parton (eds.), London: Routledge

Snitow A. et al. (eds.) (1983) *Desire: The Politics of Sexuality*, London: Virago

Tatchell P. (1992) *Europe in the Pink, Lesbian and Gay Equality in the New Europe*, London: GMP

Trevisan J. (1986) *Perverts in Paradise*, London: GMP

Viney E. (1989) *Ancient Wars, Sex and Sexuality*, Dublin: Attic Press

Waaldijk K. and Clapham A.(eds.) (1993) *Homosexuality: A European Community Issue, Essays on Lesbian and Gay Rights in European Law and Policy*, Dordrecht: Martinus Nijhoff

Walshe E. (ed.) (1993) *Ordinary People Dancing, Essays on Kate O'Brien*, Cork: Cork University Press

Watney S. (1987) *Policing Desire, Pornography, AIDS and the Media*, London: Comedia/Methuen

Weeks J. (1977) *Coming Out, Homosexual Politics in Britain from the Nineteenth Century to the Present*, London: Quartet

Weeks J. (1989) *Sex, Politics and Society: The Regulation of Sexuality since 1800*, London: Longman

Weston K. (1991) *Families We Choose: Lesbians, Gays, Kinship*, New York: Columbia University Press

White E., ed. (1991) *The Faber Book of Gay Short Fiction*, London, Boston: Faber and Faber